T0090882

THE LIFE

CHANGING

POWER OF

GOD'S LOVE

Learn how to live in the
Fullness of God's Love
Find Purpose & Meaning
Break Free & Be Healed

Sandy Baird

Order this book online at www.trafford.com/08-1554
or email orders@trafford.com

Most Trafford titles are also available at major online book retailers.

Note for Librarians: A cataloguing record for this book is available from Library
and Archives Canada at www.collectionscanada.ca/amicus/index-e.html

Printed in Victoria, BC, Canada.

ISBN: 978-1-4269-0004-4 (soft)
ISBN: 978-1-4269-0006-8 (ebook)

*We at Trafford believe that it is the responsibility of us all, as both individuals
and corporations, to make choices that are environmentally and socially sound.
You, in turn, are supporting this responsible conduct each time you purchase a
Trafford book, or make use of our publishing services. To find out how you are
helping, please visit www.trafford.com/responsiblepublishing.html*

*Our mission is to efficiently provide the world's finest, most comprehensive
book publishing service, enabling every author to experience success.
To find out how to publish your book, your way, and have it available
worldwide, visit us online at www.trafford.com*

Trafford **PUBLISHING®** www.trafford.com

North America & international
toll-free: 1 888 232 4444 (USA & Canada)
phone: 250 383 6864 ♦ fax: 250 383 6804 ♦ email: info@trafford.com

The United Kingdom & Europe
phone: +44 (0)1865 487 395 ♦ local rate: 0845 230 9601
facsimile: +44 (0)1865 481 507 ♦ email: info.uk@trafford.com

10 9 8 7 6 5 4 3 2 1

Contents

Introduction

God has great and wonderful plans for our lives. Before I came to the Lord, I felt a pull and drawing towards something I couldn't explain. At the time I didn't realize it was God drawing me to Him. When I asked the Lord into my heart, I felt a change come over me. A journey began as I grew in the Lord and was led by His Holy Spirit. The more I learned, the more wisdom, understanding and insights I received as God did an inner healing work in me. It was a process that took time as I learned to lean on God and be led by His Holy Spirit to discover His will for my life. Writing became a healing tool as I sorted out my feelings and the struggles I was going through. As God did His healing work in me, He would show me what and how to pray to break strongholds others were under so they could be set free. I found through my writing, God gave me a gift that could be used to help others gain insights and understanding for the struggles and battles they faced. I believe God wants me to share these insights and to expose the lies and deception the enemy uses to distort our view of God and His will for our lives.

Many of us live a mediocre existence never realizing our full potential or receiving the many blessings God has in store for us. Without God, we live a life of emptiness and incompleteness. There is nothing and no one that can fill the void the way God does. When we are going through trials and struggles, we often find ourselves turning to God. It is where we need to be to learn to lean on God, seeking His will and being led by His Holy Spirit. God knows us best because He made us. He gives us talents and abilities and can give us what we truly need.

We have an enemy at work that continually tries to take our focus off the Lord, causing us to settle for less than what God has for us. The enemy will use whatever means he can to manipulate and control God's children to keep them out of the will of the Father. Fear and unbelief are primary tools of the enemy. We can miss out on what God has planned for us by living in fear and not believing He can change our lives. We may resist change, letting fear and unbelief get in the way of stepping out in faith or we can chose to conquer our fears, believe God and allow His plan and purpose to prevail. The things that hold us back can be our own wills and mindsets that get in the way of what God wants to do through us. God will not override man's free will. God will however, put burdens on the hearts of people to pray for those that need healing and to be set free from the enemy. We are in a battle and until we break free from the enemy's hold, we will be in a constant struggle in our walk with the Lord.

We can be saved, but still be in bondage to hurt and pain that keeps us from experiencing emotional healing, peace and wholeness through Christ. As we follow the Lord's leading and guidance, we can learn how to change old behavior patterns and break free from strongholds. God wants us to lead full lives, set us free from bondage and experience healing for our wounded souls. We will know the love God has for us, find true freedom, peace and meaning when we have been healed and set free. Knowing and believing God loves us lays the foundation for us to have emotional healing and wholeness. When we allow God to, 7 e will do an inner healing work in us that forever changes us. Through finding the hope we have in Jesus, we can see a way out of the hopelessness and darkness many of us find ourselves in. Breaking free from bondage releases God's power and brings healing as God fills us with the desire and longing to be in 7 is will. It is up to us to accept God's free gift of salvation and seek and follow 7 im to discover the wonderful plans 7 e has in store for us. By breaking free from the enemy's hold and allowing God to heal and restore us, we will discover 7 is love and the talents and abilities 7 e's given us to live full lives. I hope and pray the insights and understanding I've learned will help others to experience healing and find freedom through The Life Changing Power of God's Love.

Chapter 1

How to Know God's Will

God made a way for us to be connected to Him through His son, Jesus. Giving our hearts to the Lord gives us the ability to communicate with God and learn more about Him and what He wants to do in our lives. It gives God great joy to see His children long to know Him and want to be in His will. God designed us to have fellowship with Him and desires to have a deep personal relationship with us. It takes time to build a relationship with God, to trust Him and learn His ways. As we study God's Word, pray and seek fellowship with other Christians, we come to know God's character and our faith and trust in Him grows. When we pray we are connecting and drawing closer to God. We'll discover God's will by seeking after Him, praying and learning to be still to listen for His response. The closer we draw towards God and pray for His will to be done, the more our hearts will be open to what He wants to do in us and we will know and feel His love.

Opening our hearts to God will help us to see the direction we are to go in for His will to be done. As God leads us, we find our desires begin to change and we long to be in His will. Our old way of living begins to lose its appeal and importance. The things we struggle to overcome, bad habits, poor behavior patterns, desires in the world that are bad for us begin to slip away. God

8

is gently influencing us to want to be in His will as we are drawn closer to Him. He works in such a way that we don't feel like we're giving up anything, we just lose interest and it feels natural. We cause unnecessary anxiety and stress on ourselves trying to rush God's process to find out what we should do or what He has planned for us. As we seek God and His guidance we can be rest assured He will lead us in the way we need to go. God will put on our hearts and minds what we are to do or where we're to be if we're unsure. God gives us wisdom and guidance when we ask for it.

> *If any of you lacks wisdom,*
> *he should ask God, who gives*
> *generously to all without finding*
> *fault, and it will be given to him.*
> *But when he asks, he must believe*
> *and not doubt, because he who*
> *doubts is like a wave of the sea,*
> *blown and tossed by the wind.*
> *That man should not think he*
> *will receive anything from*
> *the Lord, he is a double-*
> *minded man unstable*
> *in all he does.*
> *James 1:5-8*

Being double-minded is wavering between two thought patterns. It can cause confusion in our minds when we're unsure of what we are to do if we feel pulled in two different directions. As we learn to discern the voice of God, we will have peace and be more assured that we are going in the direction God wants us to go in. Knowing God's voice and having the willingness to listen and follow Him will break us free from being double-minded as we become more sure of His will. We will find our true purpose in life, one step at a time as we acknowledge God and allow His Holy Spirit to lead and guide us. We can make plans and believe things are going to turn out a certain way, but God always surprises us and they rarely turn out the way we planned. That can be a good thing because we don't always know what is best for us. God has so much more for us than we could ever imagine if we only allow Him to show us and are willing to let His Holy Spirit lead the way.

> *"No eye has seen, no ear has heard, no mind has conceived what God has prepared for those who love him."*
> *1 Cor. 2:9*

> *Many are the plans in a man's heart, but it is the Lord's purpose that prevails.*
> *Proverbs 19:21*

Our full potential may never be realized if we don't know God's will or how to find it. God designed each one of us with special gifts and abilities. We may know what our talents and abilities are and pursue them, but so often it comes through trial and error to discover what they are. As we learn God's voice and are led by His Holy Spirit, God can help us to discover the gifts He has given us. One of my favorite scriptures is Jeremiah 29:11 that tells us God knows the plans He has for us and wants to prosper us, giving us hope and a future. Those are encouraging words to live by. God wants us to explore and discover our talents, abilities and gifts He's given us. We can be blocked from seeing what they are from our own wills that can stand in the way or mindsets that have been instilled in us. There weren't the opportunities and technology in past generations that we have now. Many of us may have dreams that were repressed and never realized. We can have self-doubt, unbelief or fear of accomplishing anything worthwhile in life. Experiences we've been through or negative words spoken to us can cause us to doubt our abilities, put fear in us to try new things or believe the dreams we have in our hearts will come true. It can hinder us from taking risks and realizing our full potential. When there are talents and abilities in us that are unrealized and lie dormant, we're unable to grow and flourish becoming what we are meant to be. Responsibilities and other obligations can make it challenging when we do find what we are to do, but God is above everything and He can make a way for us to become all we can be if we trust and follow Him. When we bind up fears, unbelief or self-doubt in Jesus Name, it breaks the hold it had over us. We can ask God to breakthrough our mindsets and change our thinking. As we focus on God, we will see new possibilities and be more open to

11

them. God will lead us in a new direction to expand our horizons drawing out our hidden talents to help us to blossom and grow. We can accomplish so much if we don't allow fear or other things that hinder us from moving forward to stand in the way. Jesus came to give us life and to have it abundantly (John 10:10). Some people may mistake that to only mean prosperity and riches, but it means much more than that. God does want us to prosper, but He also wants us to grow, learn to love and to find purpose and meaning. There's nothing wrong with desiring or feeling a need to want more for our lives. It could be God putting the desires in our hearts to fulfill a deeper purpose and to give our lives meaning. We are to be content in God, but that doesn't mean He wants us to live a life of emptiness or loneliness. There are times when we feel like we're in a dark and lonely place where God has to work through our circumstances to bring into place what He has planned for us. As we look to God and give Him our lives to do what He knows is best, we will be content and have peace. Fixing our eyes on Jesus gives us hope and insights for what we're to do. When we are filled with God's Holy Spirit, our desires become what God wants for us and He gives us the strength and courage to follow Him and to do His will.

God might ask us to do things that may not make sense to us. God gives us understanding by showing us things to come in the spiritual realm of what He wants us to see (Isaiah 4J:5). We need to test the spirits to see if they line up with God's Word to know what we are receiving is from God (1 John 4:1-3). There maybe times what God shows us seems to contradict what we see in the natural realm. When we look at things in the natural we can be quick to judge without understanding what God is doing or wants to accomplish. If we feel something isn't quite right, it could be God trying to show us it's not of Him. God will give us peace and a knowing in our hearts when it is of Him. There will be times we will feel a heaviness when God puts a burden on our hearts prompting us to pray to break through any hindrances or roadblocks that could be standing in the way of what God wants to bring about. To know God's will, we have to tune into Him and learn to discern His voice. As we learn to hear God's voice and are obedient to Him, we can make those right choices that will bring us what we need and to do His will. As this is a crucial area in our walk with the Lord and knowing His will, we will discover in a later chapter how to discern His voice and the roadblocks we encounter that can hinder us from hearing Him.

Having unhealed hurts can block us from finding and knowing God's will. God wants to heal us emotionally and break us free from unhealthy patterns and strongholds. Hanging onto hurt, pain, anger, resentments, bitterness, rejection or pride can stand in the way of us coming into the fullness of God's love and of knowing and seeing His will prevail. To know God's will we have to earnestly seek it and learn to submit our wills to His will. As we learn to let go, giving everything over to God, our hearts are softened and God can do His healing work in us to accept and receive His will. We can pray for God to help us to let go of anything we are holding onto. Letting go and believing God to show us the way to go brings a true peace and knowing in our hearts and spirits and gives us confidence in the Lord. When God takes us through emotional and spiritual healing and breaking bondages, it allows us to see more clearly the direction in which we are to go in. Being in bondage puts us under Satan's influence and we can easily be deceived and distort God's will. Breaking the hold Satan has over us enables us to trust and build our faith in the Lord bringing us freedom and a closer walk with Him. God will give us the strength and wisdom we need to defeat the enemy. We don't fight against flesh and blood as it tells us in Ephesians 6:12. Our battle is in the spiritual realm. We need God's power and authority and His strength to overcome our weaknesses and to defeat the enemy. We can learn more on how to have healing and break bondages in later chapters.

Being in God's will is the only way to live in the freedom of Christ. We have to lay our own wills down to see God's will be done. God had to take the Israelites out of the bondage of Egypt (Exodus 14:21-31) and bring them into the Promise Land before they could see the freedom God had for them. He has to do the same with us. God has to take us out of bondage for us to see the freedom and abundant life He has for us. We bring glory to God by not giving up, by overcoming the battles in our minds and hearts to live a Victorious life through

Christ. We can stand firm in Christ knowing we have the Victory in Jesus to overcome all odds enabling us to know and do God's will.

Chapter 2

Trusting God & Being Secure in His Love

How do we learn to trust God and be secure in His Love? We build relationships with others getting to know them by spending time with them, listening and connecting with them. In the same way we can build a relationship with God. We talk to Him by praying and learn more about Him from reading His Word. As our relationship with God grows and we get to know Him better, we will be comforted and encouraged, knowing He wants to bless us with good things. The closer we are drawn to the Lord, the more we will be filled with His Spirit and the seeds of faith will be sown into our hearts, building our trust and faith in Him. We will have a knowing in our hearts and spirits that God loves us and has great plans for our lives. The more we understand who God is and know His character and the love He has for His children, the more we will be secure in Him.

There can be a number of reasons why we lack trust and faith in God. Abusive relationships that have caused fear, insecurity, inadequacy or feelings of unworthiness can hinder us from trusting and feeling secure. Negative words that have been spoken to us can sink into our hearts and spirits causing us to believe lies that we are unworthy or undeserving of the good God has for us. We may believe God doesn't love us enough or won't come through for us because of what we've done or of mistakes we've made in the past. When we've been hurt or betrayed, it can cause us to put walls and barriers up that leave us in darkness and blinded to God's truth. There will be a fear of trusting again, of loving someone or letting someone love us. It closes us off and we struggle with feeling or knowing God's love. It can be difficult to let go of the hurt and learn to trust again, but barriers need to come down, for us to be healed and to be secure in God. God will never turn us away, reject us, let us down or betray us (John 6:37). Those are lies the enemy tries to feed into our hearts and minds. When we've been broken and wounded, we will struggle to trust and believe until we let go and allow God to bring healing. God wants us to take a step of faith to reach out to 7im, to take hold of 7is hand, but it can be difficult when that step seems more like a leap. It's as if we're standing on the ledge of a mountaintop feeling like we're going to fall off if we let go. We can't let go until we can trust and we can't trust until we feel secure in the Lord. It is a vicious cycle that can be difficult to break free from.

Feeling undeserving or unworthy can create a block and cause us to keep our distance from God. It causes us to doubt and have fear that God won't bring us what we need or make good on 7is promises. Fear can cause us to use manipulation to try to get our way and our needs met if we don't trust God to meet them.

Fear causes us to struggle with believing and trusting God and we can doubt His love for us. If we've been taught the wrong kind of fear of God, believing we'll be punished, it'll keep us from drawing close to God. The healthy fear of the Lord is a reverence and awe and respect for God. If we have the wrong kind of fear, it's because we don't understand God's love for us. He loves us so much, He made a way for us to be reunited with the Father through 8esus (8ohn 3:16). In 1 8ohn 4:16,18, 8ohn explains how there is no fear in love because God is love. God loves us unconditionally. If we haven't felt loved through being hurt or from the pain of rejection, it's difficult to comprehend unconditional love. Truly knowing the love of the Father makes all the difference in how we perceive love and whether we're able to accept God's love for us. If we don't feel worthy, we'll reject it, we won't trust it, we'll fear it and turn away from God instead of running to Him. Living in the fullness of God's love is accepting and embracing the love He has for us. We will believe God loves us and reject the lies of the enemy that wants to keep us from knowing the love of the Father and living in the fullness of His love.

Our hearts need to be open to truly experience God's love. If we are secure in God's love and trust Him, we will be more willing to open ourselves up to whatever God has for us. We can struggle in this area when we're not sure how to trust God or be dependent on Him. Although having independence is necessary, being too independent can make it difficult to learn dependence on God and leaning on His strength. The belief we are weak if we ask for help can be a stumbling block in learning to lean on God. Focusing on our circumstances can block us from seeing a solution to problems. When our focus is on God to help us find solutions and to give us ideas, it lifts us up and broadens our thinking. If we're to go in a new direction and can't see it, God can breakthrough our old mindsets, so we can see new possibilities. We're capable of so much more, but we limit ourselves. We stay stagnant, not willing to change or grow when we don't allow God to root out fears or blocks in our minds that would enable us to see new possibilities for growth.

When our dependence is on God, we feel secure. Insecurity puts fear and doubt in us and we feel vulnerable and unprotected. Putting our security in someone or something else can cause us to be emotionally insecure or unstable. We're looking to man for acceptance and approval and to meet our needs instead of depending on God to meet them. When our security is shaken through the loss of a job or a relationship, it can cause us to fall apart. We will feel like we have lost our self worth when we have put our security in another person or a job. When our security is in God and our world collapses, we won't be left devastated when we trust in the Lord to see us through. God doesn't take away life's problems, but when we look to Him, He helps us through them giving us strength and wisdom when we ask for it. We will feel safe and secure in Him and see more clearly the direction we are to go in for what He has planned for our lives. Having our strength and security in the Lord helps us to know our value and self worth as a person. We can accept ourselves and be content in God when we know who we are in Christ. Learning to let go of the security we are putting in something or someone other than God leaves us open to the blessings God wants to bring us. Letting go removes a heavy weight and frees us. It helps us to accept and receive what God has for us whether they be challenges to help us grow, taking us out of our comfort zone or blessing us with a special person to share our lives with. We may discover a side of ourselves we never knew existed when we are willing to let it all go and give God control over our lives and circumstances. We will reject the lies of the enemy telling us we're worthless, when our security is in God, knowing we have been made worthy in Him.

It's difficult to comprehend just how much God cares for us and loves us if there are walls up in our hearts and minds. When the walls come down, we can experience and know the love God has for us. Duet. 30:6 says, 'the Lord your God will circumcise your hearts and the hearts of your descendants, so that you may love him with all your heart and with all your soul, and live.' Circumcising our hearts is vital to an intimate relationship with Christ. It opens up our hearts to God's love. It removes the layer of protection that we put up around our hearts so we won't feel any more hurt or pain, but in doing so we don't allow ourselves to feel and know God's love and the peace and joy He wants to fill it with. When our hearts are open to God's love, they are softened and pliable. God can enter in and do the mighty healing work in us that we so desperately need to be made whole in Him and be secure in His love. As we learn to trust and lean on God believing Him for His promises, the more we will be secure in Him and feel safe and protected. God's perfect love casts out all fear (1 John 4:1J). When we are secure in the Lord, we can learn to trust again and are able to love others that are trustworthy.

When our focus is on God we feel more at peace and are uplifted. It gives us hope and confidence and builds our faith. God reveals how much He loves us no matter how much we've failed or haven't measured up to the expectations of society or others or even ourselves. As we learn to trust and feel secure and safe in God, we'll find it easier to let go. When we can accept God's love and His goodness, we will be secure in the Lord knowing He will meet all of our needs according to His riches in Christ Jesus (Phil. 4:19). We will know how much God loves us and we'll be able to accept and receive the blessings He has for us. Scripture helps to encourage us when we're not able to see or understand what God is doing.

Trust in the Lord with all
your heart and lean not on
your own understanding; in
all ways acknowledge him,
and he will make your
paths straight.
Proverbs 3: 5,6

When we fix our eyes on Jesus, we step out of the natural realm and into the supernatural realm enabling us to fully trust and have faith in God. It enables us to see beyond and it gives us the courage to do what God wants us to do. As we keep our eyes focused on God and His will for our lives, it is impossible to walk in fear. Looking to ourselves and focusing on our situations can cause fear, doubt, confusion, indecision or worry. Fixing our eyes on the Lord enables us to walk in Victory instead of defeat. We become more discerning and are more in tune with God. As the truth of God's love and faithfulness sinks into our hearts and spirits we find trust comes more naturally and it builds our faith in God knowing He will meet our needs. Letting go of our preconceived notions of what we think we are to be or do with our lives, taking God out of the box and letting Him have His way frees us. God can soften our hearts and heal our wounds as He draws us close to Him until we feel safe in Him. The Holy Spirit can move so powerfully in us delivering us from hurt, fears or anything else that holds us back from knowing and being secure in God's love.

God takes us through trials to help us grow and mature. It builds character and gives us understanding that allows us to help others through their struggles. God can use our trials as a preparation ground for us to learn what is necessary for what He maybe calling us to do. Whenever we face adversity and trials, they can be an opportunity for growth and to draw closer to God, developing a deeper relationship with

Him. If we never faced trials, we would never see our desperate need for God. Looking to God to meet our needs helps build our trust and faith as we put our security in Him. God breaks strongholds over our lives and gives us strength, confidence and boldness to move forward. It is through God that we come out of trials and suffering stronger and Victorious in Christ. Trusting God means stepping out in faith leaving behind those things that are familiar and walking out into the unknown. When we read through Hebrews, it shows examples of how men of the Bible put their faith in God.

*Now faith is being sure of
what we hope for and certain
of what we do not see. And without faith it is impossible to please
God, because anyone who comes to
him must believe that he exists and
that he rewards those who earnestly
seek him. By faith Noah, when warned
about things not yet seen, in holy fear
built an ark to save his family. By his
faith he condemned the world and became heir of the righteousness that
comes by faith. By faith Abraham,
when called to go to a place he
would later receive as his
inheritance, obeyed and
went, even though he
did not know where
he was going.
Hebrews 11: 1,6-8*

Jesus came to bring salvation and to give us abundant life. Having abundant life is living life rich in love and the freedom to be who God designed us to be. We give God reason to rejoice and delight in His children when we have the desire to be in His will and learn to lean on Him. Knowing the truth of God's greatness and letting it penetrate deep into our hearts and spirits, becoming part of our beliefs, we will be secure in God's love. Without God, we struggle with doubts, anxiety, fear or unbelief about our future instead of turning to God and putting our lives in His hands. It is not always easy to do, but as we ask God to help us to stay focused on Him, we will find ourselves believing more and developing greater faith in the one who made us. Anxieties, worries and fears leave us as we learn to put our faith, trust and security in God. We will know beyond a shadow of a doubt that we are truly loved by God and we will be secure in His love.

Chapter 3

Healing For Hurt & Damaged Emotions

No one can go through life untouched by sorrow. We have all suffered from loss, heartache and pain. We may try to go through life doing things under our own strength, but God wants to show us there is a better way. God's desire for us is to be healed and made whole. When our emotions have been damaged by the hurt and pain we've suffered, it's difficult to feel whole or loved. We need healing from the hurt and pain to be able to live full lives. Learning to lean on God, opening our hearts to Him and allowing Him to heal us sets us free. Knowing and believing God loves us lays the foundation for us to experience emotional healing. If we don't believe God loves us or can heal us, we will struggle in our walk with Him and learning to trust Him.

Through the fall of man, we have been separated from God and will never feel complete or whole without Him. As fragmented human beings the void it has left can never be filled completely through another person or other things. Knowing something is missing can draw us to the Lord, making us ready to accept Christ's free gift of salvation. Receiving the Lord into our hearts changes our attitude and outlook on life. The things of the world that seemed so important to us before begin to fade. We lose the desire to stay in unhealthy relationships, wanting something more and better for our lives. We find ourselves wanting to be free of addictions that have kept us bound. As we experience God working in and through us, we respond differently to outside influences and stress. Our focus becomes more God centered instead of on self. That's not to say we aren't in a spiritual battle, for there is a real enemy at work that will continually try to take our focus off of God and lie to us. We can live our lives free in the Lord by learning how to fight against the enemy, break free from bondages and experience emotional healing. Through God's love and healing power, we can find forgiveness, peace, fulfillment and freedom from the past.

The healing process begins as we acknowledge the hurt or rejection we've gone through. God can bring healing when we let Him bring our hurtful feelings to the surface and let go of the pain it's caused us. If we don't allow the hurt or pain to surface, it hinders the healing we need to be free and to grow in God. We can ask God to root out all the hurt and pain, betrayal, rejection, guilt or shame, so He can do a complete cleansing and healing work in us. God's cleansing blood being washed over us unveils our eyes to see things that are hidden and buried deep within us, so they can surface. Praying the blood of Jesus over our minds brings clarity and breaks the confusion Satan tries to blind us with. Going through the cleansing process can bring tears of sadness and grieving. We need time to grieve, to express our pain, to shed our tears. If we don't allow ourselves time to grieve and instead repress our feelings, we can become bitter and harden our hearts. Without healing, we tend to hang onto fear, anger or bitterness that keeps us bound. Fear can stem from our past hurts and experiences we've been through. God has to root out and heal the deep-seated fears in us to be able to bring what 7e wants into our lives. Allowing the hurt from our experiences to rule us robs us from the joy God wants to bring us. Our hearts remain closed off and in a state of brokenness when we have unhealed hurts. When we are healed and free of the rejection we have suffered, we won't reject the good God has for us. God wants to fill our hearts with 7is perfect love that casts out all fear (1 John 4:1J). God can only fill us with 7is love when our hearts are open to receive. God is the one that heals the brokenhearted, binds up our wounds (Psalm 147:3), brings emotional and spiritual healing and sets us free. Emotional healing changes our hearts as we are cleansed and set free in Christ.

When our hearts have been closed off because of deep hurts we have suffered, letting go and submitting our wills to the Lord can be difficult. God has the keys to our hearts and knows how to open us up and go into the deepest, darkness corners of our hearts where our feelings can be hidden, repressed, buried and locked away. If we ask God to unlock the doors of our heart, 7e can unblock any repressed feelings and hurtful memories. They need to be brought into our awareness for us to be freed from the hurt they've caused us. It can be painful as memories and repressed feelings and emotions come to the surface, but it's necessary for the healing to come. When God takes us through a cleansing process, memories and flashbacks will surface. They need to come up for God to root them out and do a healing work in us. God wants to heal hurtful memories, regrets and mistakes from our past so we can move on and live our lives free in Christ. Letting go, giving everything over to God, allows us to experience complete emotional and spiritual healing. Problem areas will never get better until they are brought into our awareness and dealt with. We can build walls as a defense to keep the hurt and pain from surfacing, so it never has a chance to be dealt with or healed. We have to let God in and allow Him to heal us. When we let go, God can do a spiritual cleansing in our hearts and minds. We're no longer hanging on and carrying around burdens that only weigh us down and cause heartache, pain and turmoil in our lives. We become stronger and more open to receive what God has for us and are better able to cope with life. Being healed changes us. It opens our eyes to see the truth and to tune into God to hear His voice. It gives us the desire to know God and have what He wants for us. When there are deep issues that need to be dealt with and healed, God will not bring everything up all at once because He knows we would not be able to bear the depth of the hurt and pain that would well up inside of us.

*"I have much more to
say to you more than you
can now bear. But when he,
the Spirit of Truth comes,
he will guide you
into all truth."*
John 16:12,13

Although this scripture is Jesus talking to His disciples about Him going away to be with the Father, it also helps us to understand that God will only take us through what we can cope with. Once one area of our lives is healed, God can begin to work on another, taking us further and deeper to experience more healing. That's why it can takes years to go through the healing process if there are deep hurts. We may not be ready to deal with some issues that are deep rooted and God will never push us or force us to deal with anything we aren't ready to. God gently begins revealing those areas in our lives that need to be dealt with when He knows we are ready to handle them. There are times however that God will press in and prompt others to pray for us when He knows the bondage we are under is causing more hurt and pain in our lives or in someone else's life. God wants to free us from bondage and keep us from hurting more or hurting others. We will feel a need to pray and draw closer to God when He is at work in us. God's Holy Spirit will be there to comfort us through the pain. There can be heaviness and depressed feelings when things are coming up and we can feel it when God is breaking through. The heaviness lifts off of us and we will feel a lift in our spirits and have a sense of relief when strongholds are broken. God will give us peace (Phil. 4:7) and we will have a knowing in our spirits when 7 e has broken through. There is a void when something breaks and it's important to draw close to God and ask 7im to fill us with 7 is love. We don't ever want to leave ourselves open and vulnerable to the enemy. There may be more that needs to break through, but each time something breaks, God can go deeper bringing more healing. As we open up to God and let 7im in, 7e can do a mighty work in us giving us clarity and understanding as strongholds break and we are set free.

If we find ourselves stuck in the same patterns and mindsets, it can hinder us from moving forward. We may go through various relationships only to find they end up with the same results until we have healing from past hurts. Without healing, we can sabotage relationships because of our fears, insecurities and low self worth. Bringing unhealed hurts to a relationship prevents us from truly opening up and being vulnerable to another. If there is still hurt inside of us, we'll have fear of getting close to anyone else. We will never experience real love and the life God wants to give us until we can get past the hurt. We may have stubborn pride that says, 'I won't let anyone in or let anyone get close to me again'. When we've been hurt we shield ourselves by not letting God or others get too close. The shield we have put around our hearts becomes a wall we put up that no one can get passed. When we are fearful of getting hurt again, we feel vulnerable and keep closed off. We are afraid of exposing our real selves for fear of being rejected. We may hold onto the negative experiences from our past, building a wall around ourselves to keep the hurt out. We may only allow ourselves to open up to someone again if we feel safe and secure that they won't hurt us. It's like living in a shell only letting someone get close enough to form a bond without really opening ourselves up completely before we retreat back into our shell pushing them away when we can't handle the closeness. Even if deep down we desire closeness, if it scares us too much we will push others away. We can't truly give ourselves to another if we haven't been healed from past hurts. We'll hold a part of ourselves back, finding it difficult to accept or receive love. We won't let someone love us and we will find it difficult to be open enough to love others, closing our hearts off to the love God wants to bring us, settling for less than what God has for us. We may try to avoid the pain by hiding from our feelings and love staying in our comfort zone, not willing to be open to new possibilities that help us to grow and stretch as a person. We stop our potential for growth when we don't deal with our past and allow God to heal us.

We can't experience total healing without forgiveness. We carry burdens and heaviness in our hearts when we are unable to forgive. We don't realize the enormous burdens we carry when we hang onto unresolved hurt and pain. It keeps us in bondage. Not being able to forgive impairs our ability to move forward, have

31

healthy relationships and to heal. The anger and bitterness weighs us down and affects our relationships in a negative way. It can cause repressed emotions and feelings hindering God from doing a complete healing work in us. There may be unresolved issues of shame, guilt, anger or unrealistic expectations others have had on us. It can be difficult forgiving someone who has hurt us deeply. We can feel anger and rage at them for the hurt and pain they've caused. Anger and rage towards another person that has caused us hurt and pain can surface when we are reminded of it or certain circumstances trigger those feelings or emotions. It is difficult to let go and forgive, but if we don't we can remain angry and bitter, hardening our hearts. We give power to the enemy when we hold onto heartache and pain because he will use our hardened hearts to inflict pain and hurt onto others. If our hearts are hard, we lack compassion and sensitivity towards another and it can blind us to another's needs. God can soften our hearts and do His healing work in us. Hurt can cause us to hold onto anger or resentments. Letting go of the hurt helps us to be able to forgive, setting us free from what holds us back from truly loving and living our lives. It's a process that can take time, but when we are willing to be open to God and allow Him to work in us, it changes us. We can ask God to help us to let go of the hurt and pain if we're not able to. We can't try to force ourselves to forgive or rush through the process of being able to forgive. It takes time as we sort out our feelings and emotions, working through our hurt and anger or feelings of betrayal. There can be no true forgiveness from the heart if we haven't let go or worked through our feelings. We will have only accomplished shoving it down and not truly forgiving. When we allow God to soften our hearts, our hurt and anger lessens. God can then bring healing and these feelings won't be allowed to fester in our lives, carrying over to other relationships and poisoning them. As we open our hearts to God, we'll receive healing and be able to forgive a hurt, releasing the anger and bitterness. We will have and feel an inner peace and joy in our hearts when we are healed from our past and the hurt we have suffered. Total forgiveness frees us from the chains that have kept us bound and from the heavy burdens we were never meant to carry. It is God's place to deal with the other person that has hurt us, not ours. God can bring restoration and healing to our lives no matter how much hurt and pain we have been through. Forgiveness changes us as we open up our hearts to let healing take place. When we forgive someone, we feel a sense of release and peace. The anger and bitterness are gone that have held us captive. Hurtful memories are healed and we are freed from the bondage that the pain has caused. It breaks the ties that kept us bound to the person releasing us and setting us free. We will feel a sense of compassion and understanding towards someone who has hurt us that we weren't able to before. We can feel their pain and realize that they too have suffered from their own hurt and pain and need healing. If we have truly forgiven someone we will pray for them, praying a deep felt prayer that healing comes to their lives, so they'll be set free.

It's not only forgiving others that's necessary for our healing, it's learning to forgive ourselves. If we don't forgive ourselves for things we've done in the past, it can hold us back from moving forward in our walk with God. We have to remember that when we've given our hearts to the Lord, we're changed. Our eyes are open to the truth and we can let go of things we've done in the past. Jesus forgives us and He wants us to forgive ourselves. None of us are perfect and we all fall short of the glory of God (Rom. 3:23). When we're changed, we don't want to do the things we did before or live our lives the way we used to. There is no condemnation in Christ (Rom. J:1), but by not forgiving ourselves, we bring on self-condemnation. Letting go and forgiving ourselves is part of healing and being set free.

Softening our hearts and turning to God opens us up for God to do a healing work in us to make us stronger and more spiritually aware. God loves us and wants us to grow and flourish to be all we are meant to be. It does not weaken us or make us more vulnerable to hurt when we let go and forgive. When things remain hidden deep inside, it doesn't allow for healing or growth. God wants us to experiencing healing to set us free, but we have to be open to God to let Him heal us. When He roots up buried and repressed feelings, emotions and hurts we've suffered, we have to let them go to have healing. If we hold onto them after they've surfaced, we will feel heaviness because we are holding onto the burden instead of letting go and letting God do the healing work in us. We cannot experience true freedom when we hang onto past grievances and closing off may shield us from perceive hurts that we may expose ourselves to, but it also shields the good out as well. We can move passed our fears, failures, hurts and whatever else that is keeping us from living a full life when we give it over to God and are open to the love and goodness God has planned for us.

God wants His children to be free. That's the only way we will experience the life God has for us, full of peace and joy and fulfillment. We will not be able to experience all that God has for us when we are not free from past hurts. When we call on God, His Holy Spirit will comfort us and help us through the tough times by putting others in our lives to help us. We may get a phone call, encouraging us or we will feel God's warmth as He puts us on someone's heart to pray for us. If we feel heaviness in our hearts and someone is on our mind, God may be prompting us to pray for that person. We learn compassion for others as we feel their pain and identify with them in their weaknesses. We can learn valuable lessons and can gain insights and understanding when we go through pain and suffering. We can learn new ways of coping, of communicating and find new patterns of relating. It can be a long and painful road, but when we are done, we'll be able to truly live the life God has meant for us to live. After we have gone through a time of healing we experience growth and have a more mature walk with the Lord. When God heals us of our hurts, we can receive wisdom and insights that allow us to move forward and it give us the tools to help others to heal and move forward in their lives. We receive emotional and spiritual healing when strongholds break and we develop a sensitivity and compassion for others from the hurt we've been through. It enables us to help others when they go through similar hurts.

God wants us to experience love in our lives, the deep profound love that He has intended for us. It is a part of who we are and how God made us because He is love. We need the wholeness and healing in God to be able to love unconditionally and allow ourselves to be loved in the way God designed us to be. God gives us unconditional love and the assurance that He loves us no matter what. Only through releasing everything to God can we be healed and made whole. We have to want to be free of those things that hold us back and allow God to take us through the process of helping us to heal. There maybe times we find that being alone with God and going deeper in Him is the only way for us to experience true healing. Life and people can distract us from what we need to focus on to allow God to root up feelings and emotions that can be buried deep within us. Being alone for a time can be painful, but as God does His healing work in us, it frees us from past hurts and the bondages that we've been under. When we have the love of Christ in us, we'll be able to receive love and love others unconditionally. We will be able to live full, complete and satisfying lives and have our deepest needs met. We'll become the person God has intended and meant for us to be when we are healed and made whole and complete in Christ.

Chapter 4

Letting Go, Surrendering Our Wills to the Lord

Surrendering our wills to the Lord allows healing to flow and opens the doors for God to bless us. The healing brings us freedom from the hurt and letting go releases God's power. Letting go is the key to total emotional and spiritual healing because it allows God to work in us without our wills getting in the way to bring about what He desires. It breaks the hold the enemy has had over us and he loses the control to hold us captive and in bondage when we willingly give our wills over to God. When we allow God free rein, He can root out everything that is standing in the way of what He wants to reveal to us and accomplish through us.

There can be many areas we struggle with in being able to let go and trust God completely. Until we put our security in the Lord, we will find it difficult to let go and put our trust and faith in God. Fear, unbelief, doubt, worry or rejection could be some areas we battle with when trying to let go. It takes courage to be able to let go, but as we do, revelations, insights and answers come to problem areas we may have been struggling with. God can supernaturally break through the powers of darkness when we let go of whatever holds us back from putting our faith and trust in God. As we let go and learn to lean on God, our faith grows and so does our conviction to do God's will. We will have the desire to walk in God's Spirit and in His ways. When we are able to totally let go giving everything over to God and relinquishing control into His hands, we will see His power move mightily in our lives for His will to be done.

We know there is a battle going on in our minds, but what is in our hearts can affect our thinking. The way we think and our reasoning can stem from hurt and pain or rejection we may harbor in our hearts. When we've been hurt, we tend to put walls up in our minds and close off our hearts, stubbornly resisting God's Holy Spirit. Hanging onto hurt, anger or bitterness causes distorted thinking and allows the enemy to come in and create strongholds in our hearts and minds. We need to let go of whatever we are hanging onto that causes doubt, unbelief or fear. Disappointments, regrets or negative thought patterns can also play a role in our ability to be open to God. Negative thoughts can stem from patterns we've learned or from disappointments or rejection we've experienced. We'll struggle to fulfill God's plan and purpose if we're bound up in old patterns of thought and negativity. God needs to break down the walls and barriers that keep us prisoners to the past and hold us back from living fulfilled lives. God wants us to be free and cleansed from anything that holds us back from us living a life filled with purpose, meaning, love, joy, peace and fulfillment. Binding up the strongholds in Jesus

Name loosens the stronghold and God can root out all the negativity in us. The rejection we have suffered from, our doubts, unbelief and fears will begin to disappear as we let go, giving them over to God. We will see our lives change, as we lay our lives down at the Lord's feet.

Many times when we're waiting on God to breakthrough, we find He is waiting on us to be ready to face or deal with our issues. There could be areas of pride or fear in us when we don't want to give control or our wills over to God. God is waiting on us to let go, to trust Him completely. Letting go helps us to see what we need to pray or do for the breakthroughs to come. Our hearts can feel heavy when we struggle with things we can't seem to get passed. We need God's divine intervention to break us free for our circumstances to change. Trying to do it on our own can cause us to grow weary when the battle becomes too great and we want to give up. God doesn't want us to give up and shrink back in defeat, but if we give the battle to Him to fight for us, God can work it out in His way and in His time. We may not be ready to completely surrender our wills to God until we feel overwhelmed by life. It's often in times of desperation that we call on the Lord for deliverance from our troubles. God will help us to let go when we reach out to Him. When things are beyond our control and we can't see how our circumstances can possibly change, it's then God can show His glory turning everything around to His good. God can change our lives when we are willing to yield and submit our wills over to Him. God has the power and ability to change our circumstances and to move in people's hearts to bring into our lives what He knows is best for us.

"For my thoughts are not
your thoughts, neither are
your ways my ways,"
declares the Lord.
Isaiah 55:8

Satan can keep us blinded and distort our thinking causing us to believe we are in God's will when in fact the situation we find ourselves in could be keeping us from God's blessings. It can hinder us from seeing what needs to be changed. As we submit our wills to God, we can ask Him to show us through His eyes what we need to see. God can show us through a dream or vision or image to give us more understanding so we will know how or what to pray to break through the strongholds Satan has over us. As we grow in the Lord, we gain more wisdom and understanding of the spiritual realm and are better prepared to fight and do spiritual warfare. We will feel God's prompting to pray when He wants us to do battle in the spiritual realm. There may be weariness when we are fighting the battle, but there is also a peace and sense of relief and a renewed hope as we feel a weight come off and a lift in our spirits as things breakthrough. We feel a change inside as we let go, giving us more discernment and a knowing in our hearts and spirits that we are in God's will. God brings us into a deeper relationship with Him as we learn to walk in His Spirit.

God has a plan and purpose for our lives. We have to give up the control that we think we have to see God's plan unfold. God knows what's ahead and the steps we need to take to get there to become the person He has designed for us to be. If we let stubborn pride get in the way that says 'I want to do it my way,' it can create hardships and delay the blessings God wants to bring us. Unless we totally surrender our wills to God and release our lives and circumstances to Him, we may miss out on the life God has for us. He knows what is best for us, whether it's the kind of work we're suited for or the person that He knows is right for us. God will not override man's free will, but He will gently move in our hearts to soften them to help us to let go. God will show us how to let go if we don't know how to. We may have to let go of the life we're living so God can bring us the life we were meant to live. God will continue to knock on the door of our hearts until we let Him in and let Him take over, so we can see His plan and purpose unfold.

"In his heart a man plans his course, but the Lord determines his steps."
Proverbs 16:9

"Many are the plans in a man's heart, but it is the Lord's purpose that prevails."
Proverbs 19:21

There is a peace that comes with surrendering our wills to the Lord. It lifts the heavy burdens off of us, freeing us and leaves everything in God's hands, where it rightfully belongs. We will feel the weariness when we're letting go and releasing our burdens to God. It's like carrying a heavy load for miles until it becomes too heavy for us to carry any longer and we stop and put it down to rest. Only with God, we need to leave it there because it's 7 is to carry. God can move mightily to change our circumstances when we let go. We are drawn closer to God as we learn to let go and become more dependent on 7 im. All the clutter and baggage we have been carrying around with us into relationships and our work place needs to be gone for us to live our lives free in Christ. We may lose the security of a job or a relationship because God has something better for us that we can't see if we are hanging onto them. God may have a greater purpose and calling for our lives that we may not understand or come to know unless our security had been shaken.

Surrendering to God doesn't mean that 7e controls us, but rather it frees us. Man's need to control is a stumbling block and hindrance to what God wants to do. Until we learn to let go and let God take over, we will never know the extent of God's power (Gen. 1: 3-27), what 7e is able to do and the love 7e wants to show us. Complete surrender to God is the only way we will experience true freedom in Christ and the love God has for 7 is children. When we learn to let go and trust God, we often find an inner strength we may never knew we had. We don't do things under our own strength, but as we look to God, we find our strength in Him. As God brings us into maturity, we find ourselves more content and have greater wisdom and understanding. We can thank God after for putting us through the trials and tribulations because what comes out of it is wholeness in God, healing for our emotions and being able to let go of the past. God moves in our hearts to make those changes within us that are needed to make us whole and complete in Him. We are changed for the better and are able and ready to move forward. We are free from the hurt and patterns that can cause destruction in our lives and keep us bound. It is in the place of complete surrender when we stop striving, worrying and fretting that we find peace and discover God's will and the direction we need to go in. We are able to accept and receive what God has for us and stop resisting and fighting His will out of fear or not feeling like we deserve it or can measure up. When we give it all over to God, He can turn our lives around and give us purpose, meaning, peace, joy and fulfillment. God can make something beautiful out of our lives when we let go and learn to lean on Him.

Surrendering our wills is being willing to die to self. Submitting our wills to the Lord is saying yes to God that we're willing to do it His way and follow Him. Dieing to self, giving of ourselves, every fiber of our being over to God allows us to go deeper in God. We grow in God as we allow Him to take over, giving Him more of ourselves. In giving God the control, Satan loses the control he has had over us. If our faith is weak, our spirits will cry out to want to be in God's will, but our flesh can rise up when we feel vulnerable or fearful (Gal. 5:17). The battle for wanting to stay in control can be so strong we can struggle to let go and lay everything at the foot of the cross and say yes to God. When we give God free rein to take over, we will find it easier to be led by His Holy Spirit. Letting go is how we win the battle in our hearts and minds so we can see God's glory and His plan unfold. As we give everything over to God and allow Him to heal us, we will be freed from the strongholds that have kept us in bondage and chained to our past.

Chapter 5

Blocks to Hearing God's Voice

Learning to hear God's voice is a process that takes time. There has to be a willingness and our hearts open to hear God's voice, but it can become a struggle if we try too hard. We will learn to discern God's voice as we draw closer to Him through prayer and taking some quiet time after we've prayed to listen. There will be a peace that comes over us when we are hearing God's voice. He gives us insights, revelation and wisdom to help guide us in whatever we're to do. If God is prompting us to make changes in our lives, He will never do it in a way that puts pressure on us. If we're feeling pressure or negative thoughts come to our mind, it isn't coming from God. God will never pressure, rush or push us into a situation before we're ready. He will always prepare our hearts before leading us in whatever we are to do. Learning to discern the voice of God will help us to discover God's will and His plan and purpose for us.

If we find ourselves struggling or have trouble hearing God's voice, there could be problem areas that are blocking or hindering us from hearing or recognizing the voice of God. We may not know how to reach out to God or to put our dependence on 7im if we're too self-reliant and trying to do things under our own strength. 7aving legalistic beliefs or living under the law can cause us to struggle in this area. We may do what we think we should do, instead of learning to lean on God and listen to 7im. It can cause wrong thinking if we believe we have to prove we're worthy of God's love instead of living in Christ's freedom and knowing we are made worthy in 7im. In James 2:17, it teaches us that Faith by itself is dead without works. Doing what God wants us to do is the best way of showing our faith in 7im. In James 2:21-23, Abraham put his faith into action by being obedient to God and doing what was asked of him fulfilling scripture and making his faith and actions complete. 7e was not being self-reliant. 7e was looking to God and seeking 7is wisdom and guidance, being obedient to the Lord.

If we are unable to hear God when we are sincerely trying to, there could be controlling spirits at work. Rebellion and disobedience are controlling spirits that could be at work in us that can block us from hearing God. Being in rebellion can cause a resistance to authority of which God is the ultimate authority figure. Resistance to authority can keep us from hearing God if we stubbornly insist on doing things our own way and tune God out. Our hearts have to be open and receptive to hear God and being in rebellion closes our hearts to God. Rebellion, disobedience and wanting control all have pride in them. Going our own way and not being obedient can cause us to make choices that are out of the will of God, leaving us open to deception. Satan wants us to remain in the dark, continuing to rebel and be disobedient to God, so we don't turn to God and seek His wisdom and guidance (8ames 1:5). Disobedience can be attributed to not having the fear of the Lord in us. We often lack the understanding of why it is so important to learn obedience and having the fear of the Lord. God only has our good in mind and we can be so easily led astray when we're not walking in obedience to God or showing respect for Him. Binding up rebellious spirits that resists the voice of God, opens our spiritual ears to be able to hear and discern His voice.

"Let the wise listen and
add to their learning and
let the discerning get
guidance."
Proverbs 1:5

"The fear of the Lord is the
beginning of knowledge, but
fools despise wisdom
and discipline."
Proverbs 1:7

Another area that can cause problems in hearing God is we have hardened our hearts. It may be caused by pride, rebellion or hurts we've been through and we find it difficult to open ourselves up to hear God's voice. We may not understand why we're unable to hear God's voice if we are sincerely trying to. Our hardened hearts and unhealed hurts become a block and a wall goes up coming between God and us that shuts God out. Closing our hearts hinders our walk with God and being able to listen to hear His voice. Struggling with self-doubt and unbelief can be major stumbling blocks in learning to listen and to hear God's voice. Pride, rebellion, fear, stubbornness or an unwillingness to change are other obstacles that stand in the way of us discerning the voice of God. God could be trying to speak to us, but if there is fear, unworthiness or other things standing in the way, it will block out His voice. If we're not ready to accept or receive what God has for us, we may subconsciously tune Him out. We have to be ready to receive. God has so much for us if we are only willing to accept the good He wants to give us. If we don't learn to listen to God, it is difficult to know what He desires for us or the direction He wants us to go in. It is a ploy of the enemy to keep us blinded, in fear or believing lies to keep us out of the will of the Father. The Holy Spirit spoke through Isaiah to God's people admonishing them, wanting to give them understanding of the importance of softening their hearts toward God. We can ask God to soften our hearts so we can hear and receive what He has to say. When our hearts are soft, they're pliable and yield more easily to God's Holy Spirit. We become open to God and more willing to submit to Him.

'Go to this people and say,
"You will be ever hearing but
never understanding; you will
be ever seeing but never

*perceiving." For this people's
heart has become calloused; they
hardly hear with their ears. And
they have closed their eyes. Other
wise they might see with their
eyes, hear with their ears,
understand with their
hearts and turn, and
I would heal them.'*
Acts 28: 26,27

Pride can be a major block to hearing God's voice. Pride will cause us to resist the 7oly Spirit because we think we know better and want to do things our way. It hinders us from listening and wanting to hear God's voice. Pride becomes an obstacle in us learning what God wants to teach us. In Acts 7:51 a prophet speaks to the people of Israel calling them a stiff-necked people with uncircumcised hearts and ears that causes them to resist the 7 oly Spirit. When our hearts and ears are not cir-cumcised, it means they are closed. Our hearts are not open to receiving the Word and our ears are not open to hear God's voice. We can get caught up in our own agendas and what we think God wants instead of listening and truly seeking after 7 im and 7 is will. To truly know God's will and to follow it, we need to let go of our pride and humble ourselves and allow God to lead us in the direction 7 e wants us to go in. 7aving a humble heart makes us more submissive to God's 7oly Spirit and enables us to be more open to 7 is leading and direction. We are called to be more like Jesus. What better way than to be cloaked in humility. Jesus 7imself stepped down from glory, cloaked 7imself in humility, became poor and went through human suffering. 7e wants us to let go of our pride, to become like 7im, so that we may be able to share in 7is glory (Romans J:17). God wants to reveal 7is plan for us, but we have to be willing to listen and be obedient to 7im to be able to see and accept and receive the good 7e has for us. We can ask God to circumcise our hearts and ears so we will be able to hear 7is voice and be more open to 7is leading and guidancc. By allowing God to root out the problem areas, we become more discerning and are able to hear God's voice clearer. When the rebellion and pride goes and we have a teachable spirit, we will be able to gain the wisdom and guidance we need to know God's will. As God draws us to 7imself, 7e softens our hearts, breaking down any stubborn resistance, giving us the desire to hear and follow 7im. God is so patient with us. 7e will wait on us and keep knocking on the doors of our hearts until we let 7im in. Our lack of understanding at the awesomeness of God can be a factor in not listening to God or having the desire to live for 7im. 7e has the power to do whatever 7e pleases, but 7e will never override man's free will. 7e is a gentle and loving God who only wants what's best for us (Matt. 11:29). When we fear the Lord and reverence 7im, we will want to be obedient to 7im and do what pleases 7im. We will come to understand that what 7e wants to do in our lives benefits us. If we truly understood that, we would let go of our resistance and submit our wills to His. Having a submissive spirit towards God and being able to hear His voice allows us the privilege of getting to know the Father and the wonderful plans He has for our lives. We only need a willingness to listen to God and an open heart and spirit to discover and experience the good gifts God wants to give His children.

Chapter 6

When We Give Our Hearts to the Lord

We can be drawn to God in any number of ways. We may realize our need for God through suffering, loss or trials we've faced. It could be from someone witnessing to us that opens our eyes of understanding to see our need to be saved. No matter how we've come to the Lord, we soon begin to see and understand the significance of our decision and the change it has made in our lives. When we've given our hearts to the Lord, we have made the choice to accept Jesus as our Lord and Savior. We have willingly made it known that our desire is to follow God and be in His will. When we've chosen to give our hearts to the Lord, God's Holy Spirit comes to live in us, filling us with the desire to want to become more like Jesus. God wants us to live a life pleasing to Him, to keep us from harm and protect us from the enemy and to bring us blessings. God knows we need to have emotional healing to move forward to live our lives free in Him. He wants to heal our hurts and free us from anything that keeps us bound. God desires to accomplish great things through us, to help show others their need for God and to see them set free from the strongholds the enemy can have over their lives.

God made us and has a plan and purpose for our lives. When we become Born Again by giving our hearts and lives to Jesus, it changes our thinking and our desires. God works in us to bring about what He longs to give us. God is the one that gives us gifts, talents and abilities to give our lives meaning and for what He has purposed for us to do. We can't do it on our own or under our own strength. We are not meant to. God wants us to learn to lean on Him and His strength. God doesn't expect it to come easily for us, but when we are willing to humble ourselves and ask for God's help, the more we become like Jesus and will receive the blessings God has for us.

"I am the vine; you are the branches. If a man remains in me and I in him, he will bear much fruit; apart from me you can do nothing."
John 15:5

Jesus is the vine and He is our lifeline. If we don't remain in Him, we are cut off like the branches that come off a tree. The branch by itself withers and dies. When we don't know Jesus, we are like a branch that has no life in it. The fruit Jesus talks of is the everlasting fruit, the kind that makes a difference in our lives and in the lives of people we touch to bring them into the knowledge of knowing Christ as their Lord and Savior. When we make the choice to give our hearts to Christ, God will help us to follow Him. In 1 Cor. 6:19,20 it says,

"You ar; not our own; you w;r; bought at a pric;." Onc; w;'v; giv;n our h;arts to th; Lord, God will h;lp us to l;ad th; liv;s H; int;nd;d for us to l;ad, a lif; pl;asing to Him. God wants to k;;p us fr;; from th; ;n;my and out of bondag;. Wh;n w; hav; giv;n our h;art s to th; Lord and ar; not walking right in Him or living th; way w; should, God may hav; to disciplin; or corr;ct us to k;;p us from b;ing d;c;iv;d . W; may still b; caught up in th; bondag; to sin and J;sus wants us to b; fr;; from th; sin that so ;asily ;ntangl;s. Th; word disciplin; can carry a n;gativ; connotation. Having th; und;r-standing that God wants to k;; p us from harm and fr;; from th; ;n;my h;lps us to gain a b;t-t;r p;rsp;ctiv; on th; conc;pt of disciplin;. W; can ;v;n b; thankful that H; car;s ;nough for us to want to t;ach us th; right way to liv; .

> *"My son, do not make*
> *light of the Lord's discipline,*
> *and do not lose heart when he*
> *rebukes you, because the Lord*
> *disciplines those he loves and*
> *he punishes everyone he*
> *accepts as a son."*
> *Hebrews 12:5,6*

> *Our fathers disciplined us*
> *for a little while as they thought*
> *best; but God disciplines us for*
> *our good, that we may share in*
> *his holiness. No discipline*
> *seems pleasant at the time,*
> *but painful. Later on,*

however it produces
a harvest of righteousness
and peace for those who
have been trained by it.
Hebrews 12:10,11

God wants us to live lives pleasing to Him so we can share in His glory and the many blessings He wants to give us. We hinder the blessings God has for us if we're going in the wrong direction or doing things that are causing us harm. When we are caught up in sin, we are where Satan wants us to be. We are not free spiritually or emotionally and are unable to lives our lives free in Christ or to do the work of the Lord effectively. As Christians, we lack credibility and the power and authority we have in Christ when we aren't living right in God. We can be Born Again and know Jesus and still feel lost. Sin puts a distance between the Lord and us. Nothing can separate us from God's love, as it states in Romans J:39, but we put a wall up between us and the Lord that causes our relationship with Him to suffer when we are in bondage to sin. God wants us to be free of sin so we can live our lives free in Him.

"Let us throw off every-
thing that hinders and the
sin that so easily entangles
and let us run with perseverance
the race marked out for us. Let us
fix our eyes on Jesus, the author
and perfecter of our faith, who
for the joy set before him

*endured the cross, scorning
its shame and sat down at the
right hand of the throne of God.
Consider him who endured such
opposition from sinful men, so that
you will not grow weary and lose
heart. In your struggle against
sin, you have not yet resisted
to the point of shedding
your blood.*
Hebrews 12:1-4

This scripture is encouraging us to stay away from everything that hinders our walk with the Lord. Not resisting to the point of shedding our blood means we are not seeing the significance of what Jesus did for us on the cross. We may still be doing what we please, instead of living to please God. God loved us so much, He made a way for us to be saved and reunited with the Father. Salvation washes away the sin and does a spiritual cleansing in us, opening our eyes to the truth.

*This is how God showed
his love among us: He sent
his one and only Son into the
world that we might live through
him. This is love: not that we
loved God, but that he loved
us and sent his Son as
an atoning sacrifice
for our sins.*
1 John 4: 9,10

We live in darkness when we don't know 8esus and we're not following Him. It can be easy to get deceived and fall prey to the enemy and get caught up in the world's ways. Satan will come against God's Word and His truth using lies, deception, fear, doubt and unbelief causing confusion trying to prevent us from fulfilling what God has planned for us. The enemy will use whatever means he can to try to distract us away from what God has for us. God will give us the strength and ability to break free from the enemy when we call on His Name. 8esus came to bring us freedom and to walk in Victory. He will never put us to shame or condemn us. There is no condemnation in Christ for those who have given their hearts to the Lord (Rom. 8:1). It's the enemy that causes us to feel shame or condemnation. God will help us to rise up against the enemy of our souls and walk in His ways and in His strength. When we resist the devil, we aren't allowing him to have power or dominion over us. God wants to cleanse us and make us whole in Him. Spiritual cleansing breaks bondages that can blind us to the truth. We can ask God to cleanse our hearts, minds, eyes and ears to expose the lies of the enemy and the deception we are under, so we can be set free. As we lean on God and His strength, our spirits rise up, our faith increases and we close the door on the enemy.

God can reveal things to us through a feeling or knowing in our hearts or spirits to help us learn discernment. Although we aren't to rely on emotional feelings, the God given knowing or instincts we feel is different and should not be ignored. It could be warning us of danger or to keep us from emotional harm. Having sensitivity to feelings is not a bad thing. Women tend to be more intuitive and often times it's through feelings that we sense things that maybe wrong or that might put us in danger. The enemy may try to lie to us making us believe we are weak when we feel things deeply. We are human and if we shut that part of ourselves off, we deny a part of who we are. Our feelings or instincts are there to tell us something and God can use them to help guide us. We need to be careful of our emotional feelings that can change, but we have to be open and sensitive to God's leading and the knowing He puts in our hearts. God could be prompting us to pray for someone or giving us direction. Of course it is wise to pray and confirm what we are feeling to see if it is from God or our own emotions we are acting upon. Asking God for revelation knowledge and being led by His Holy Spirit will help us discern the difference and to stay in His will, knowing what is being revealed to us is of Him. Testing the spirits (1 John 4:1-3) will help us to know and stay in the truth.

God can give us revelations or insights through dreams or visions of what He wants to reveal to us. God gives us visions and dreams for more than one purpose. He may give us a vision or glimpse into the future of what He is preparing us for or wants to bring us. As we seek God and pray into what He has given us, we can have the assurance He is at work to bring about what He desires in His time and His way for His will to be done. God will use dreams or visions to encourage us when we are being plagued by doubts or unsure of which direction to take. He may show us roadblocks or obstacles in the way that we need to pray against. We can ask God to interpret our dreams for us if we're not clear on what they mean. God may give us warning dreams when He wants us to pray against something that He doesn't want to see happen. It maybe to advert disaster or to pray to move in another person's heart to help guide them in making a right decision that God wants for them. God will call on His prayer warriors to pray for others and for their situations to bring about needed changes in their lives or to avoid something bad happening. We may not always see the good our prayers have accomplished, but we can be rest assured they were necessary if God has called us to pray.

When we are walking with the Lord and He calls us to do something for Him, we need to remember to put our armor on (Eph: 6:11) and pray the blood of Jesus over us whenever we do anything for God. God will always protect us so no harm comes to us if we are diligent and remember to pray the protection around us and bind up Satan's attacks. We also need to bind up sabotaging spirits that will try to come up against what God wants to accomplish through us. Satan will use fear, doubt, confusion, frustration or indecision to try to block and sabotage us. Stepping out in faith and battling against the enemy will provoke attacks. Satan is scared and angry and knows he's defeated, but we still have to do our part and pray the blood covering over us. We need to pray a protection around our loved ones as well because Satan will try to attack them if we don't pray God's protection over them. We never want to leave ourselves open and vulnerable to the enemy. God will help us in our weaknesses, giving us strength and power over the enemy to fulfill His plan and purpose. It is up to us to remain in God, seeking to stay free from sin and cleansed through the blood of Jesus. As we seek to do God's will, we know we can trust Him that He will lead and guide us and follow through with what He has given us. We need to keep our hearts open to God, allowing Him to work in and through us, being led by His Holy Spirit, so we can accomplish mighty things for His Kingdom.

Chapter 7

Repentance
Sets Us Free

Repentance is having a change of heart and mind. We may long for something better when the way of life we're living no longer holds the appeal it once had. Repentance releases us from the damaging effects of sin and the guilt and shame it leaves in its wake. It sets us free from our past. It allows God to cleanse us, giving us a fresh start, to turn from our past, our failures and old way of living to learn a new and better way. Being in sin leaves us open to deception and the lies of the enemy. Much of the oppression we are under and the shame and guilt we may feel is caused from the damaging effects of sin. Like Adam and Eve in the Garden of Eden, they felt shame and hid their faces from God when they knew they had done wrong (Gen. 3:J). Shame and guilt can cause us to feel unworthy to come to the Lord. If we find ourselves still being plagued by shame or guilt or anything else after repenting and giving our hearts and lives to Jesus, it could be we're not letting go. Satan is never happy when we have been set free and will use our past against us feeding us lies that we are unworthy and don't deserve to be free. The fear or lie that God will punish us can block us from entering into 7 is presence. When we call upon the Lord, He will deliver us from the lies, our fears, unworthiness or anything else that stands in the way of us drawing closer to God.

If we're struggling to give up our old way of living to follow Jesus, we may not be giving our lives completely over to Him. God knows our weaknesses and wants to help us break free from self-destructive behaviors. Things may keep going wrong before we see our need to change and turn to God or be willing to ask Him to help us to change. We may have the desire to know God and want to live for Him, but don't know how to ask for help or to let go and give everything over to Him. God will help us when we ask and He will show us how to let go of whatever we are hanging onto that is keeping us from experiencing true freedom in Christ. God will prompt others to pray for us to help us to turn to God, to give us strength to resist the enemy and to set us free. God may need to break down walls we've put up and any pride in us, humbling us to melt the hardened shell we may have put around our hearts to help us to be free. When our hearts are harden, it causes us to stay blinded and under the deception of the enemy. Satan wants to keep us in bondage to fear and feelings of unworthiness, so we will not cry out to God in repentance and come into the freedom of Christ. When God breaks through barriers and walls we have put up, He can move freely in us opening our eyes to see the truth. Truth sets the captives free (John J:32). God opens our hearts to understand, so we are able to live our lives free in Him. God immerses His cleansing blood over us freeing us from bondage, breaking down the walls and our defenses, softening our hearts, so we can be filled with more of Him. When we're not filled with God's Spirit, we tend to follow our own desires and the ways of the world and walk in the natural realm instead of walking with Christ in the supernatural realm. Falling under the powerful anointing of the Holy Spirit causes us to cry out to God, to want to be set free and to see our lives changed. When God's Spirit pours over us, we find the struggle is gone as our attitudes change and we no longer want to live the way we have been living. We are changed as God does a healing work in us, restoring us making us whole. The light of God's truth penetrates deep down into our hearts, minds, spirits, souls and wills. Our spirits rise up, resisting the enemy when God delivers us out of darkness, weakening Satan's influence as we gain Victory over our lives.

Repentance breaks through the lies and deception of the enemy and brings us into the freedom and knowledge of Christ. We will know God works for the good of those who love Him (Rom. J:2J) and wants what's best for us. It frees us from the guilt and shame Satan tries to keep us bound under and frees us from our own condemnation that can keep us from drawing close to God. The Bible teaches us that there is no condemnation in Christ (Rom. J:1). We can come to God freely and He forgives us no matter what we have done. The cleansing power of the blood of Jesus frees us and releases us from all unrighteousness. We know that we are forgiven and worthy in Christ. The Holy Spirit helps us to renew our minds and to break us free from wrong thinking and wrong beliefs.

*Those who oppose him he
must gently instruct, in the
hope that God will grant them
repentance leading them to a
knowledge of truth, and that they
will come to their senses and
escape from the trap of the
devil, who has taken them
captive to do his will.*
2 Tim. 2: 25,26

*Whoever finds his life
will lose it, and whoever
loses his life for my
sake will find it.*
Matt. 10:39

We like to think we have the control, but not following Jesus leaves us open to being influenced and controlled by the enemy. Rebellion is a controlling deceptive spirit that has its roots in pride and needs to be broken, so we can see our need to repent and turn from our own ways. Breaking free from our rebellious ways, repenting of our sin and turning away is dieing to self as we give our lives to Christ. Dieing to self and our old way of life simply means we are no longer allowing ourselves to stay in bondage to sin. We are accepting and acknowledging that living our lives free in Christ is a far better way to live then being under bondage and believing the lies of the enemy.

For we know that our
old self was crucified with
him so that the body of sin
might be done away with, that
we should no longer be slaves
to sin, because anyone who
has died has been
freed from sin.
Romans 6: 6,7

God wants us to live in the light of 7 is truth and 7is Word. If we ask God 7 e will shine 7is light into us piercing through the darkness into the deep recesses of our minds and hearts where we may have things hidden and buried. God brings them up to the surface to be dealt with (Luke 8:17) and to bring us healing. When we come into the place of true repentance, it means we are ready and willing to change and accept God's will. It's making a decision and choice to follow 7 im. Letting go of our pride and truly repenting can cause us to fall to our knees, bringing an end to our self-defeating ways. We will be released of the guilt, shame or condemnation that we may have felt and have been hanging onto setting us free in Christ. Repentance humbles us as we learn to let go and surrender our wills to the Lord. It cleanses us and lifts a weight off of us as we come into the righteousness of Christ. God will give us the desire and ability to do 7 is will when we turn to 7im. We will see a change in ourselves as God turns our lives around. When we admit we can't do it on our own, admit our failures and our weaknesses, it's then that God can truly work in our lives and turn them into something worthwhile. We find we no longer have a distorted view of God or have a fear of coming to Him. We can let go of any wrong beliefs and the fear or lie we are weak if we lean on God. We become strong when we lean on God's strength because it's through God's power that we gain Victory over our circumstances and over the enemy. It's only through true repentance and turning from our own ways that we can be totally set free in Christ and free to be able to live the abundant life God has desired and purposed for us to live.

Chapter 8

When It Feels like God is Not Enough

There's something inside of us that will never feel completely whole or fulfilled when we don't have God in our lives. There's a void in us that can't be filled with anything this world can offer. God meets all our needs according to His riches in glory. (Phil 4:19) That's His promise to us. God fills an empty place in our hearts and souls. He is our source and provider and gives us unconditional love. It is through God that we receive blessings whether they be financial or bringing us someone to share our lives with. He puts creative ideas in our hearts and minds and provides us with opportunities for growth. God opens doors for us by influencing others to show us favor for work or things we have need of. God will work through people and circumstances to bring us what we need and for everything to fall into place for His plan and purpose to unfold.

Our love for God doesn't mean there won't be times we go through dry spells in our relationship with Him or with others. We can feel disconnected at times and empty and alone when we are going through pain, suffering, loneliness, rejection or loss. We all go through difficulties and have unanswered questions in life. It's not easy to see how God can be enough for us when we're going through struggles or heartaches or that He has a plan for our lives when we can't see the bigger picture like He can (Isaiah 46:10). Our emotions can overwhelm us at times and we may feel like we're failing God. It's not wrong to feel God is not enough or that we should be made to feel guilty or that we're failing God when we feel that way. When we're hurting or grieving, all we can feel is the pain we are going through. Experiencing heartache and loneliness can cause us to draw closer to God. If we didn't go through struggles and hurt and pain, we would never see our true need for God or allow Him to take us through the healing process making us whole and complete in Him. God understands when we feel alone and He will help us through our troubling emotions. God's Holy Spirit gives us strength, comfort and peace as we go through our times of grief and trials, suffering and loneliness. God will take us through a time of healing if we have been hurt from relationships or other events that have happened in our lives. We will have difficulty in relationships and being able to trust others if we don't allow God to heal us. We will never be able to fully trust another until we learn to trust God. There is no way to hurry this process and all we can do is press in and pray and ask God to help us to have faith and trust in Him as He does His mighty work in us. It is often times through our suffering that God works in and through us helping us to grow, making the necessary changes in us to bring about what He desires. God will help us to see what areas in us need strengthening, giving us the ability to make the changes we need to build our faith in Him. Giving our wills and lives over to God, changes our hearts and helps us to grow both emotionally and spiritually.

"As we draw close to God,
He draws close to us."
James 4:8

When we're going through trials, it helps to have support through the church to encourage and uplift us. God intended the church to be not only a place of worship and fellowship, but to minister to those that are hurting and in need. We are truly blessed when we have God and other Christian brothers and sisters to help us through difficult times. Feelings and emotions can be overwhelming at times and we need each other. God will move in the hearts of other Christian brothers and sisters in Christ to be there for us and pray with us to give encouragement and support. God heals our hurts and our hearts, but it is a process that takes time. When we are hurting, we can become vulnerable to even more hurt and pain. We need to guard our hearts against the enemy of our souls that would try to inflict more pain on us. It can come through another person's careless words or from our own condemnation. It's important when we're ministering to others that we encourage and uplift someone in pain and not discourage or discount their feelings. Having compassion, sensitivity and understanding helps others when they are going through trials. We can learn much through pain and suffering if we don't allow it to make us bitter. God can use our suffering and the struggles we've been through in ways we may not yet comprehend to help others in whatever they are going through. When we've gone through a time of healing, we have more understanding of what God was doing, enabling us to move forward being more willing to step out in faith when God calls us to. Our faith in God fills us with confidence and we know we can trust 7im to meet our needs and to lead and guide us. When we arc fillcd with God's love, we can give more of ourselves and learn to love unconditionally.

It is not always easy to follow God, learning to put our trust and faith in 7im. We are human with all its shortcomings and weaknesses. We all have sinned and fallen short of the glory of God (Rom 3:23) and feel the sting of guilt and failure. We need God to complete us and make us whole to fill the void in us that only 7e can fill, but 7e also made us with an innate need and longing to be accepted, to belong and to be loved. Adam walked with the Lord in the Garden of Eden, but God knew it was not good for man to be alone and 7e made Eve for Adam (Gen. 2:18). We're not failures for feeling the need to want someone to love and be loved by, when it's a need God has put in us. We need God's love in us to fill the void in us left from the separation from God after the fall of man, but we also need God's love in us to be able to love another unconditionally. God didn't design us to live our lives alone. God designed us and puts needs and desires in us and wants to show His love to us by fulfilling those needs. God designed marriage for us to be connected and bonded with another and to create a family unit. If He has put that desire in our hearts, there will be a part of us that won't feel whole or complete without the bond and connection with the person God made for us and for the love He wants to bring into our lives. It can feel like God is not enough when our hearts feel heavy and ache and long for the very thing God has put in our hearts to have. In our human thinking we cannot totally perceive how God can put everything in place for all our needs to be met, but that is why we are called to put our trust and faith in Him. In time, we will see the outcome of the things God has promised us and wants for us (Heb. 6:15). Having trust and faith in God makes us feel secure and gives us a knowing in our hearts that He will bring us what we need to complete and fulfill our deepest longings. As we wait for God's blessings, He is preparing us for the things ahead, strengthening us helping us to grow. God will lead us to pray for Him to put everything together. God wants to fill us with His love and heal our hurts and broken hearts. God can bring people who are healed and made whole together in unity. When two fragmented hurting people come together that have not been healed and made whole in Christ, they bring their unresolved hurt and pain into the relationship causing more hurt in each other. We need to allow God to take us through the much needed healing to live our lives free in Him. It can take time as God works through circumstances and people to put everything into place. God gives us grace and mercy through our times of weakness and 7e is always there to forgive us when we humble ourselves before 7im.

God is enough for us because of who 7e is. God can do what no human being can do. God became man and walked the earth as Jesus to be our Savior, to free us from the bondage of sin, so we can be reunited with the Father in 7eaven. Jesus is the way, the truth and the light (John 14:6). There is no one else that can save us (Acts 4:12). Without Jesus, we walk in darkness. We live in light and truth and reality when we have the Lord in our hearts and in our lives. God can breakthrough wrong beliefs or mindsets that can keep us stuck going in the way we think we should go (Proverbs 16:25). God is the one that breaks through the lies and deception of the enemy setting us free. God heals us and fills us with 7is love and peace (1 John 4:15-1J). God is our source and gets great joy in meeting and fulfilling our needs. As we grow in God, we will discover the meaningful life 7e has waiting for us. We can have a peace and knowing in our hearts and spirits that God is at work to bring us who and what we need to fulfill our lives. The peace and knowing gives us the ability and patience to wait on God. When we feel a closeness and bond with the Lord, we will have an incredible peace and be content in 7im. We can feel God's love penetrate deep into our very souls. Everything else seems to fade away when we are in the presence of our Lord. When we feel God's love so strong, we have the assurance that 7e will bring about what 7e has promised and purposed for us. The best kind of love comes through God as He enables us to put others before ourselves, learning to love unconditionally.

Chapter 9

When God Calls Us

God made us with a built in need and desire to feel needed and to fulfill a purpose. Many will strive to find it, but it's through following God that we find true satisfaction and fulfillment. God is the one that made us and knows what we need. We can't escape God's calling, but why would we want to? What God has planned for us has a promise of fulfillment and joy that only He can bring. God made us to have fellowship with Him, but He also has a plan and purpose for our lives. God tells us if we have faith in Him, we will do greater things then He has done (John 14:12). How can that be? In our human understanding and limited thinking we may have a difficult time grasping hold of the possibilities of what God can do through us. We may not be able to see or fathom the life God has designed for each and every one of us. We can get sidetracked or deceived by the enemy and fall short, being disappointed when we can't accomplish on our own what we've set out to do and purposed in our minds. Humbling ourselves before God and letting go of what we think we want changes our focus. We will see our lives and other people's lives transformed and changed as we allow God to work through us to see His plan fulfilled (Isaiah 4J:3). We know if God is calling us, He will give us the ability and desire to bring about what 7e wants to accomplish through us. By fulfilling God's calling, we will find meaning and our purpose in life. We should consider ourselves privileged if God is relentlessly pursuing us because it means 7e has something special planned for us. So why is it that our human nature so often resists and fights God's calling?

We at times feel like we're in a tug of war and in a sense we are. God wants us to be free and Satan is trying hard to keep us bound. God's calling over our lives can leave us feeling isolated and alone if we aren't following the norm or what society expects of us. We can feel like we're being pulled in two different directions, worrying about what others think or fear they will reject, criticize or judge us. To follow God, we have to let go of our preconceived notions of what we are to do or what others think we should be doing and let God be our guide. If others try to discourage us or have us believe we aren't hearing God right, we only need to draw close to God and keep holding onto what 7e has given us. As God's 7oly Spirit leads us, we will have a knowing in our hearts and spirits when we are going in the right direction. God knows the steps we have to take, the things we need to go through or lessons we need to learn to obtain what 7e desires for us. God will make a way for us to do what 7e calls us to do even though we can't see what's ahead. We have to be willing to let go of our hopes and dreams, our fears, anxieties and insecurities and give them over to God and trust and follow 7im. As we open ourselves to God, 7e will help us to let go of everything we are hanging onto, so we can be ready and willing to follow our calling.

When God calls us, it can mean there will be sacrifices we have to make. Many may say it's a test of our faith, but it's more than that. God wants us to grow and that means taking us out of our comfort zone where we feel safe. It can be scary being put out on a limb for someone else, but that's often what God calls us to do. There maybe some that walk away from God's calling if they are not willing to sacrifice themselves for the sake of others, but that's what Jesus did for us. He made the ultimate sacrifice and to be more like Jesus, we are called to do the same. When God calls us, He has a specific purpose in mind. God wants to use us to make a difference and to bring others into the Kingdom of God. It's not the numbers we bring to Christ, because no matter if it's only a few, it will have a domino effect. When someone comes to the Lord, it creates a chain reaction bringing others along the way. It's not the number, it's what we're willing to do for God and the sacrifices we're willing to make that count. That is a true test of our faith and our belief and trust in God. God calls us into a deeper walk with Him to show others the sacrifice He made for us. Are we willing to do that, to give of ourselves to show God's love and draw others to Christ? If God gave us abundant life without us learning what it is to sacrifice for another, would we be able to truly appreciate what He has given and done for us? Would it make us less compassionate or insensitive to the plight and hurt and pain of others if we never had to experience trials to learn compassion and to make us stronger in the Lord? Learning to sacrifice for others humbles us and teaches us what it is truly like to be a faith believing Christian.

There can be other reasons that can cause us to struggle with accepting God's calling. When there is fear in us, we may try to run from God's calling. When we've been hurt, we may fear the feelings of vulnerability and dependency on God and we keep ourselves closed off to 7im. The hurt and pain we've been through can cause us to build walls to shield and keep us safe, but they also keep us from experiencing the life God has for us. Keeping a part of ourselves locked away and hidden so others can't see the real us puts us in a state of denial. Walls become a block to following God, denying and rejecting what 7e wants to do through us. Satan can blind us and use fear, feelings of unworthiness or lies to try to keep us from what God is calling us to do, pulling us further away from God's perfect will. Prayer releases God's power to work when we are struggling with issues and need God's divine intervention to help us to make changes or to set us free. God can break down walls and defenses we've put up and soften and melt our hearts, so we let down our guard to allow 7im do the work 7e needs to do. We lose the desire to run and hide as we fall helplessly into the arms of the Father, asking for forgiveness and mercy as we let go and become willing to answer God's call.

Another area of our struggle may be that we are in conflict of what we want and what

God knows is best for us. Resisting and running from God's will causes our hearts to be heavy and depresses our spirits. Trying to live our lives contrary to God's will is like swimming against the tide and it will cause us to feel weary and heavy laden because we are not doing what God has designed for us to do. We may be afraid of stepping out into the unknown, especially if it involves making changes. Things may continually go wrong as God tries to get our attention to lead us in the right direction. There is a pressure that will build up inside of us that we as human beings won't be able to withstand, when God is trying to get our attention to lead us in a new direction. God will call upon His prayer warriors to pray for us when God wants to move in our hearts. God won't give up on us. His Holy Spirit will continually work in our hearts to help us to be ready to accept His will and the change He wants to make in us. God wants us to come to Him and let go of any heavy burdens we're carrying, so He can give us rest.

"Come to me, all who
are weary and burdened,
and I will give you rest. Take
my yoke upon you and learn
from me, for I am gentle and
humble in heart, and you will
find rest for your souls. For
my yoke is easy and my
burden is light."
Matt. 11: 28-30

God may need to bring us to the end of ourselves, stripping away the things that are not of Him, to teach us dependency and draw us into a more intimate relationship with Him. By taking from us what we thought we wanted, God can bring us what we need. God will use our situations to show us we can't do it on our own and He doesn't want us to. God may take us through trials or tribulations that aren't pleasant. We may not understand at the time what He's doing or why. Later on however, we can see there were lessons we needed to learn for our growth and maturity and were necessary to become who God has intended for us to be. God will always bring us through miraculously, glorifying His Name to bring about what He wants to accomplish when we are willing to put our trust and faith in Him and respond to His calling.

> *I make known the end*
> *from the beginning, from*
> *ancient times, what is still to*
> *come. I say: My purpose will*
> *stand, and I will do all that I*
> *please. From the east I summon*
> *a bird of prey; from a far-off land,*
> *a man to fulfill my purpose.*
> *What I have said, that will*
> *I bring about; what I have*
> *planned, that I will do.*
> *Isaiah 46: 10,11*

This scripture shows that God has a greater purpose and plan for our lives and He will work in us to fulfill His purpose and to show His glory. God draws us in and softens our hearts so we stop resisting His Holy Spirit and the work He wants to do in us. It's through God's constant pressing in, knocking on the door of our hearts until we open up and let Him in that we will be able to accept and receive the blessings He wants to give us. God takes things away that aren't good for us so He can bring us something better. By being in God's will, we will experience the life He has designed for us to live. We can be more effective for Christ, enabling us to do God's ministry work to lead others into salvation and freedom in Christ when we have been set free. God wants to break down the walls in our minds and hearts so we can experience the fullness of His love. We can fulfill our purpose and make a difference in other people's lives by helping them to see how they can experience God's love and freedom in Christ. We may not always see God's hand at work, but according to scripture we know He is doing a work in us and for us.

> *"We know that in*
> *all things God works*
> *for the good of those who*
> *love him, who have been*
> *called according to*
> *his purpose."*
> *Romans 8:28*

God can breakthrough those dark areas in us that need changing when we let go of our wills and put our focus on Him. God does a humbling work in us as He turns us around to go in the direction He wants us to go in. Willing to let go and say yes to God with whatever He calls us to do changes us. Even if fear comes in, we can let it go and resist it, having the purpose of mind that says, ' it doesn't matter what I want, it's what God wants that is important.' When we can learn to let go and are willing to let God have His way, we will discover the possibilities and accomplish more then we could ever dream of. It changes us as it brings us into a more mature and closer walk with the Lord.

God will draw us close to Him and by His Holy Spirit we will feel moved under His powerful presence to want to follow Him and be in His will. There is something inside of us when we are called by God that explodes with an intensity and desire to fulfill what He has put in our hearts to do. We will sense a deep closeness with God as He pours out His Spirit and fills us completely with the need He's put in us for what He wants to accomplish through us. It consumes our entire being and engulfs us as our hearts overflow with God's powerful anointing to fulfill the purpose He's set our before us.

"For I know the
plans I have for you,
plans to prosper you and
not to harm you, plans
to give you hope
and a future."
Jeremiah 29:11

God fills us with a conviction and determination in our hearts and spirits, giving us the courage and strength to follow Him and the ability to accomplish His will. There will be a confidence, assurance and desire that will rise up in us to want to follow God and take the necessary steps needed to fulfill our calling. When we're walking in God's Spirit and His strength, we will feel His powerful anointing come over us. God has given us each gifts and talents to be used to reach our full potential and for the purpose of bringing others into the Kingdom of God. As God breaks through the mindsets, fears and anything else we maybe hanging onto that holds us back, we will experience an incredible peace and joy as we watch God's plan and purpose unfold. What God has in store for us is like nothing this world could ever offer (1 Cor. 2:9,10). All we need is willingness and a submissive heart towards God and say yes to what He is calling us to do. God can change lives and the more people that are willing to answer the call of God, the more lives we can win for Christ and bring others into His Kingdom and truly make a difference.

Chapter 10

God Prepares Our Hearts

God always prepares our hearts for whatever He asks us to do or wants to bring into our lives. What God asks of us and the journey He takes us through can come with many twists and turns. God would never ask anything of us if He didn't intend to bring us through miraculously, bringing glory to His Name. My journey of faith and the longing God put in my heart was nothing like I had ever imagined. It's been a test of my faith as I went through times of grieving, sorrow and turmoil mixed with hope as I longed for God's will to be done. When I knew something broke through, I would feel a sense of relief, a peace and knowing in my heart it was drawing closer, only to get thrown back into the battle I was fighting. I often felt like I was on an emotional roller coaster. So many times I wanted to get off, but felt God pulling me back, the Holy Spirit prompting me to keep praying and fighting for what God had for me. It wasn't always easy finding confidence and hope fighting spiritual battles, whether they were my own or praying for someone else God had put on my heart. So many times I found writing to give encouragement and hope to others difficult when it seemed so fleeting in my own life. Often what I felt to write didn't always reflect what my own life looked like. When at times I felt overwhelmed, God would give me reassurance through dreams, giving me a glimpse of what He had for me or what He wanted to do in my life. The dreams and visions God gives us can be prophetic. It inspires us when God speaks to us through dreams of what His will is for us. It is not only to encourage us, but also to show us what we need to pray for God to put everything together to achieve His perfect will. We can persevere, knowing the battle we're in will come to an end and God will have the Victory and bring to pass what He has promised.

Our walk of faith isn't always easy. It is in fact one that can come with many challenges and difficulties. It is probably why the road to life is narrow and few find it (Matt. 7:14). Following God doesn't come with a road map. It's not always easy to see the way we are to go or what God has planned for us. If it were simple, maybe more would chose to follow. It's sometimes difficult to comprehend God's ways or how He works through us for His plan and purpose to unfold. We can only lean on God and ask Him to help us to understand and trust Him that He has a greater purpose through whatever He asks of us. We can find encouragement in this scripture that reveals God has everything worked out ahead of time and knows what will take place. God knows the perfect time when He has prepared our hearts for what He has and wants to bring about.

*I foretold the former
things long ago, my mouth
announced them and I made
them known; then suddenly
I acted, and they came
to pass.
Isaiah 48:3*

As we go through spiritual battles, God is strengthening us, helping us to be ready, preparing our hearts to accept and receive what He has for us and wants to accomplish through us. God prepares us by first planting a seed or dream in our hearts. God will water and nurture the dream or desire He plants in us, until it grows, matures and blossoms like a flower that has come into full bloom. We may feel an emptiness or loneliness when God creates a hunger inside of us and a deep longing and desire that fills our hearts and consumes our being until what God has ordained comes to pass. The waiting can often bring pain and heartache as we hunger for the very thing God has put in our hearts. The need and desperate longing causes our hearts to cry out to Him as we press in and pray, waiting for God's plan to unfold.

*"Hope deferred makes
the heart sick, but a longing
fulfilled is a tree of life."
Proverbs 13:12*

Whenever God puts a desire in our hearts, it comes with His promise that He will bring it to pass in His time and in His way. As hard as it is to wait on God, our faith is built up by holding fast to 7 is promises and believing for 7 im to bring it about (7 eb. 11:1). Even if circumstances look bleak and the opposite of what God is telling us, we can be assured that what 7 e's given us, 7 e will do. If God has given us a promise and we are waiting, trusting, putting our hope in God, it is easy to get discouraged and fall into despair when it appears as though nothing is happening. Sometimes the wait can be long and the promise 7 e's given us seems slow in coming. We can grow weary in our wait and it can cause our hearts to feel heavy. God's 7 oly Spirit will bring us peace and comfort as we wait. In the times we feel alone we can look to God, leaning not on our understanding, but keep praying, trusting and believing in what 7 e's given us will come to pass. Focusing on God and not on our circumstances gives us hope to carry on, looking ahead to what God has planned for us.

> *"Trust in the Lord with all*
> *your heart and lean not on*
> *your own understanding, in*
> *all ways acknowledge him*
> *and he will make your*
> *paths straight."*
> *Proverbs 3:5,6*

We need to guard our hearts, as we wait patiently for God's perfect will (Romans 12:2). Satan wants to rob us of our joy and hope in God and tell us lies that God won't come through for us. Satan is a deceiver and will try to put doubt in our minds and discourage us, feeding us lies that can cause us to lose hope and the vision God has given us. Believing lies can leave us open to deception and controlling influences to operate in our lives without our being aware of it. Satan will attempt to shake our faith in God and try to steal the dreams God has put in our hearts. 7e puts doubt in our minds that we're hearing God's voice or tries to convince us it's not good for us even as God is at work to bring about what 7e desires. God doesn't want us to give up on our dreams, but to place them in 7is hands for 7im to work out. 7e knows what needs to be done for 7is purposes to be accomplished. God is a God of hope and if 7e has given us a promise, 7e is fully capable of bringing it to pass (7eb. 11: 7-12). God always has our best interests in mind and we can't always see that clearly in the midst of trials and tribulations or when we are caught in the snares of the enemy. 7olding onto our dreams and letting go of the doubt and lies releases God's power and Satan loses his hold over us. We will have a peace and knowing in our spirits that God's Word is true and 7e is able to give us what 7e's promised.

"Then you will know the truth and the truth will set you free."
John 8:32

"The thief comes only to steal and kill and destroy; I have come that they

*may have life, and
have it to the full."
John 10:10*

God is always at work in us to help us to become all we can be. 7e gives us visions and prophecy of what is to come and directs and molds us into the person we need to be to fulfill 7is plan and purpose. God gave Joseph dreams of what 7e had planned for his life (Gen. 37:5-10). Joseph went through trials and ordeals before he saw the dreams God had given him come to pass. Joseph's brothers betrayed him (Gen. 37:19-23) after he had shared the dreams God had given him. While Joseph was working as a servant (Gen. 39:1-6) he was falsely accused and thrown into prison (Gen. 39:19-23). The Lord was with him and granted him favor in the eyes of the prison warden, who put him in charge of the other prisoners. Joseph knew God and recognized 7is hand at work and held onto the dreams. In Gen. 41, Pharaoh had a dream he didn't understand. 7e released Joseph from prison after learning he could interpret dreams. After Joseph interpreted Pharaoh's dream, he put Joseph in charge of his palace and the whole land of Egypt. After seven good years there was famine in the land. Joseph's brothers came to Egypt to buy food (Gen. 42) and later his father came. The dreams God had given Joseph years before came to pass. Through Joseph's trials, God was strengthening him and refining his character to make him into the great leader God had ordained him to be. We may not understand why we go through some trials, but we can be encouraged and assured that through them, God is at work building our character and refining us to bring about what He has purposed. As God takes us through the necessary steps, we can embrace what He wants to do and allow Him to make changes in us. God knows the steps we need to take to refine and mold us to become what He has destined for us to be. A lot of the experiences we go through, even mistakes we've made can be steps or lessons we needed to go through to bring us toward the goal God has in mind for us. It's a process that's needed to help us to grow and to build our character to be all God wants us to be. When we're not ready or feeling unworthy with what God has put in our hearts, He will help us work through our uncertainty to bring us into a place of acceptance, preparing us to receive.

*"A man's steps are
directed by the Lord's.
How can anyone under
stand his own way?"
Proverbs 20:24*

*"Many are the plans in
a man's heart, but it is
the Lord's purpose
that prevails."
Proverbs 19:21*

God wants us to be content in Him, but there are times when we may feel a need for change. God doesn't want us to be complacent,

He wants us to keep growing and maturing in Him. If we are feeling dissatisfied with our lives, there may be a reason and we shouldn't ignore it or feel guilty about it. If we are happy where we're at, we would never feel compelled to make the necessary changes that God may want for us. God takes us beyond where we're at into a deeper relationship with Him. God could be preparing us for a work He has for us to do or to go in a new direction for His purposes to be fulfilled. If God didn't plant a seed or desire in our hearts, we wouldn't have the drive or motivation to go forward in Him or take the steps we need to make a change. We will feel God's prompting as He directs us in the way He wants us to go. God may open the doors for a certain job for us to meet someone or to make a difference in someone's life. The job could be a training ground for the ministry work God has for us and we may learn some valuable lessons and insights we might not otherwise learn. God has a purpose for us being there that we may not understand or see at the time. God will use jobs or experiences to strengthen us and to help us learn how to be dependant on Him before He places us in ministry. If God puts a longing in our hearts for ministry work, we need to allow God time to train us up, learning how to do spiritual warfare to fight against the enemy. Our battle is not against flesh and blood (Eph 6:12), so we need to learn how to do battle in the spiritual realm. If we don't allow ourselves the time it takes to learn how to come against the enemy, we set ourselves up for failure. God wants to equip us to have Victory in Jesus. Going through trials and facing adversity only serves to makes us stronger. We need to learn how to be strong in the Lord and operate in God's strength, not our own, allowing Him to work in and through us to defeat the enemy to see others set free. We need to be prepared and have the necessary tools to do His work effectively. He is a gentle God and will never force us into anything we are not ready for. God knows what is good for us and will gently move upon us and work in our hearts to prepare us for the plan He has for our lives. When we give our wills and lives over to God, He will work in us changing our hearts, helping us to grow emotionally and spiritually. God helps us to see what we need and the areas in our lives that need strengthening and changing for His purpose to unfold.

As God prepares us, He may prompt us to pray or to do something for Him and other times He will call us to be still and know that He is God (Psalm 46:10). We can learn valuable lessons from people in the Bible. Doing things on our own like Abraham and Sarah did, can cause heartache and grief. God had made a promise to Abraham and Sarah that she would have a child. Sarah knowing she soon would be past the age to have a child didn't want to wait on the promise or believe it would happen and did things her own way that resulted in her maidservant giving birth to Ishmael (Gen. 16: 15). The Lord had said, "his hand will be against everyone and everyone's hand against him, and he will live in hostility toward all his brothers" (Gen. 16:12). God's promise eventually came to pass and Sarah gave birth to Isaac (Gen. 21:1-3). It brought glory to God's Name because it happened when Sarah was past childbearing age and accomplished what God desired. We have to let the awesomeness and power of God sink into our hearts and spirits believing that 7e can do the impossible (Luke 1:37) as we place our hope and trust in 7im. When we look to God and seek 7im, 7e can show us a glimpse of the future when 7e has put a desire in our hearts. God can speak to us through dreams and visions, giving us insights on how to pray or give us words of encouragement if we are struggling with doubts or unbelief. God would not put us through trials unless there was a reason for it. There are times that only through the trials we go through where we are feeling most vulnerable and dependent on God and hurts buried deep surface that we see our desperate need for God. God uses our trials to help prepare us for something more or a ministry work 7e is calling us to do. God wants to strengthen us through trials to build us up, to make us strong where we are weak, so we don't leave ourselves open to Satan's attacks. We need to be strong in the Lord because whenever we do something for God and 7e is moving in us, Satan is always ready to attack any weak areas in us. That is why is it so important to allow God to do 7is work in us and let 7im prepare us for what 7e has for us. We set ourselves up for the attack of the enemy if we rush ahead of God's timing or before 7e has properly prepared us for the work 7e is calling us to do. When we give our lives to God, 7is

Holy Spirit reins in our hearts. As we earnestly seek God and His will for our lives and what He wants for us, the desires He puts in our hearts will grow. God wants us to live full and complete lives and in doing so we can make a difference in other people's lives. When the wait is over and God produces the miracle He has promised us, it brings fullness and life and as a result forever changes us.

God wants to bless others and if we're willing He will use us to help other people's dreams be realized. God may put a word on our hearts, a prophecy of what is to come that He wants us to speak out to prepare someone's heart for something special He has planned for them. When we speak prophecy over someone it brings life to the words and seeps into the person's spirit and heart and begins to take root. We need to be discerning and ask God for confirmation before we speak to someone to be sure it is of God and be careful of the words we speak as to not cause fear in them. God will not give us negative words, but always encourages us, speaking words of truth. God maybe calling them into a ministry and is using us to help them discover their calling. We need to be discerning and listen and wait for God's perfect timing, as He knows when that person will be receptive to hear it. If a person's heart is hard, they may turn in anger or be fearful if they are not ready to accept and receive. We need to pray for their hearts to be softened and receptive and wait patiently for the prompting of God's Holy Spirit to speak through us. God wants them to receive the prophecy and He will give us what we need to pray as He softens their hearts to receive. It allows God time to work in a person's heart and spirit to receive what He wants for them and to help build their faith. God knows what needs to be done and He will put on our hearts what we are to pray so He can move in their hearts for His glory to be shown. We as Christians can pray on behalf of anyone God puts on our hearts. We will see God's plan and purpose come to pass in our lives and in the lives of people we pray for when we are willing to wait and earnestly press in and pray as God's Holy Spirit prompts us, being obedient to what God calls us to do.

Chapter 11

Fasting & Prayer: The Key to Breaking Through

Prayer changes us. The more we pray, the more we're drawn to the Lord as it deepens our faith in Him. Prayer connects us to God and unlocks the doors of our hearts so God can enter in and do a mighty work in us. When we pray, we're drawn into the presence of the Lord and can sense His love. A peace comes over us as we pray giving us a knowing in our hearts that God cares for us and wants to helps us. He's concerned with every area of our lives. We can lose out on the blessings God has for us when we don't look to Him for wisdom and guidance. Fasting along with prayer draws us into a deeper relationship with God. It is an amazing tool that can be used in spiritual warfare to breakthrough strongholds in our lives and in the lives of people we pray for. Fasting is always beneficial even if we don't know what to pray. Insights and revelations often come to us after our fast. Fasting is an effective way to unblock stubborn mindsets that can stand in the way of our seeing what needs to be prayed to see breakthroughs. God works in and through us to change our circumstances when we fast and pray. God will prompt us to pray what we need to for His plan and purpose to come to pass. Our prayers do make a difference. Prayer changes our hearts and causes us to look outside ourselves to someone else's needs. God wants to change our hearts to heal and free us and to give us the desire to see others healed and set free. We can pray for our families or anyone else God puts on our hearts for Him to move and make changes in their hearts and in their lives. God gives us a compassionate heart for others, so we will feel the need to pray for them. As God prompts us to fast and pray for others, He gives us revelation and knowledge on what needs to be prayed to break them free and to bring healing. Many of our prayers God may have prompted us to pray could be to avert some tragedy. The more submissive we are to God's Holy Spirit, the more in tune we will be with God and His prompting for what needs to be prayed. When we're unwilling to pray, we in a sense tie God's hands because He won't go against man's free will. This gives the enemy the upper hand because he doesn't play fair. To gain Victory over our situations, it is imperative to learn the significance prayer and fasting can have in winning the war against the enemy.

Through fasting and prayer, we gain understanding and receive insights and revelations we might not otherwise receive. We tap into a deeper level of awareness in the spiritual realm and discover things that may have been hidden in the subconscious mind. As those things are brought to light and into our awareness, we can deal with them and be set free of the hold they've had over us. We can receive wisdom and guidance on anything we maybe struggling with and needing revelation in. We may discover realization of talents and abilities we may never knew we had. As we draw closer to God through our fasting and prayer, we learn to surrender more fully to Him as our desire for His will grows. Fasting opens up a deeper part of ourselves and we are able to focus more on God and what He wants to reveal to us. God unlocks the key to our hearts and brings us into a sharper focus as we yield to His Spirit and are able to rest in Him. We can be praying about one thing and the Holy Spirit comes over us and we find ourselves praying about something else. God may call us to rest in Him as He does an inner work in our hearts to bring healing. There maybe hurts and wounds that need to be healed that will allow us to move beyond what we wouldn't otherwise be capable of without God's healing. God does an inner work in us to strengthen us, preparing us to do battle in the spiritual realm. We will feel a prompting when it's time to pray and do spiritual warfare to break down strongholds and barriers that maybe hindering us from having what God wants to bring us. We may not fully comprehend the benefits fasting and prayer can bring, but it releases something inside of us drawing us into a closer bond with the Lord. As we are drawn closer to God, we experience peace and contentment in Him and we know we are protected against the enemy.

Spiritual warfare is hard work and can bring on weariness. God knows we need Him to go before us praying for strength to win the battle over the enemy. The 7oly Spirit gives us wisdom on how and what we need to pray to break down the walls that can keep us blinded to the strongholds the enemy may have over us. Ephesians 6:12 describes clearly that our battles are not in the physical realm. We can gain understanding and see the importance of why we need to learn how to fight the battles in the spiritual realm if we are to see breakthroughs. Fasting and prayer gives us the upper hand and one more tool to fight against the enemy of our souls.

*"For our struggle is not
against flesh and blood,
but against the powers of this
dark world and against the
spiritual forces of evil in
the heavenly realms."
Eph. 6:12*

As we go deeper in God, we are drawn closer to 7im. Our prayers become more intense and the 7oly Spirit is able to penetrate into our hearts and spirits bringing us clarity of mind. God reveals 7imself more to us as we are drawn into a deeper walk with 7im. The more we fast and pray, the more our faith is built up. God can reveal areas in our lives we struggle with to show us what needs to be prayed. Fasting and prayer dispels the darkness, as God reveals and unblocks what is hidden and breaks down strongholds. In Matthew 17:14-20 Jesus demonstrates the need for strong faith belief in seeing people delivered from controlling spirits that can hold them captive to Satan. In Matthew 17:1J Jesus rebukes the demon and the spirit comes out of the boy.

> *Then the disciples came to*
> *Jesus in private and asked,*
> *"Why couldn't we drive it out?"*
> *He replied, "Because you have*
> *so little faith. I tell you the truth, if*
> *you have faith as small as a mustard*
> *seed, you can say to this mountain,*
> *'Move from here to there' and it will*
> *move. Nothing will be impossible*
> *for you, but this kind does not*
> *go out except by prayer*
> *and fasting."*
> *Matthew 17:19-21 KJV*

Controlling spirits can be deep rooted and passed on through the generations. When we have deep hurts, it can cause us to be closed off and we may inadvertently shut God out. It leaves the door open for lying spirits or fear or bitterness to come in and take hold if we aren't careful. There can be a number of spirits operating that can have control over us causing a block to us seeing the truth and being able to do God's will. Lying spirits can keep us blinded and under deception. Spirits of fear can keep us from moving forward in God and having what 7 e desires for us. Allowing a spirit of bitterness to take root can cause our hearts to be hard. Stubborn pride can rule us and we may have an unwillingness to be open to God's 7ol y Spirit. We need to be open to God to be able to see the truth and know what needs to be prayed to see breakthroughs and live our lives free in Christ. Fasting and prayer breaks the hold controlling spirits can have over us. Through our fasting and prayer, God can reveal the deep root of our problems. God tears down walls that have been built up in our hearts and minds so He can set us free. Hurt and pain and memories from our past have to surface so God can root them out and bring us healing. He helps us to let go of them to free us from the hold they've had over us. When we aren't healed from the past, we stay stuck and there is no change and no growth. God's healing changes us and gives us the ability to move forward in Him.

We can pray and fast on behalf of others for them to be set free from generational bondages and hurts that they need healing from. God will prompt us to pray by burdening our hearts for others. We may feel a type of grieving for the person as we pray for them, knowing they are lost and hurting. God has us feel their hurt and pain to feel compassion for them, causing us to want to pray more. We can gain understanding and receive valuable insights and knowledge that can help us to have compassion, understanding and forgiveness for others as we see strongholds break and their lives changed. God may give us a glimpse into the spiritual realm of what the problem area is. Others maybe in a situation that can feel like a prison to them and they can't see the way out. God may prompt us to speak truth to them to break through the lies and deception they maybe under. Truth always breaks deception, but it is important to be led by God's Holy Spirit and not speak out prematurely. We need to pray for God to prepare a person's heart so they will be ready to receive the truth. If a person's heart is hard, they will reject the truth if they are not ready to face it.

Fasting causes us to see our true and deepest needs. Satan is a master at deception and blinds us to our true needs. Satan will use our weaknesses against us trying to pull us away from God. Prayer and fasting draws us back and we cry out to God seeking His face and direction for our lives and for breakthroughs to come. There maybe lies we have believed that cause us to distort God's will. As we fast and pray, lies can be exposed and brought up from our subconscious mind and into our awareness. Satan loses his hold and power over us when we bind the lies up in Jesus Name. Through fasting and prayer we open ourselves up to the Lord, allowing Him to do an inner work in us. God may need to unblock areas in us that we have closed off so His Holy Spirit can move freely in and through us to accomplish what God wants to do. Fasting unblocks obstacles that can be hindering and hiding the truth that needs to be revealed. Walls of defense we may have up can be a form of protection and refuge of safety from getting hurt again, but those same walls can become a prison we use to hide behind. They keep us chained to our past and fears if we don't let go of them. Every time we fast, we break through a wall or a piece of a wall and a window of light opens up and shines in and we get a glimpse into the spiritual realm. We receive revelations, gain understanding, wisdom and answers to what needs to be prayed for our circumstances to change. We get more clarity and understanding as hindrances and obstacles are removed and our mindsets are changed. God wants us to be free and bless us, but He first has to break through, so we can receive what He desires for us. Through fasting and prayer we can see strongholds shatter as we find total freedom and healing in Christ.

Fasting makes us more spiritually aware and we are able to discern and interpret things more easily. Fasting and prayer brings spiritual truths and pierces through the darkness, breaking down walls and loosening the enemy's hold. Satan may use fear to blind us and we may be unwilling to acknowledge the truth and to face issues that are painful. We can fall prey to deception caused by our own failures and weaknesses. We have to want to be free from our past before we can face the future and deal with whatever we need to. We have to remember to be on guard against the enemy. Satan will try to come in with lies trying to convince us our prayers aren't working and that we don't need to fast to see breakthroughs. We can shut the enemy out by binding up the lie in Jesus Name and keep praying until we see the breakthroughs and God's will come to pass. It's through our fasting and praying that allows God's hand to move in and through us to bring change. God takes us into a place of total and complete dependency on Him in order to root

out whatever is in us that hinders us from becoming who 7e has designed us to be. It builds
our faith, strengthens and draws us closer to
God when we continue to fast and pray.

The revelations and insights don't always
come the day we fast. Sometimes it will pop up
into our awareness in the middle of the night or
in the next day or so. It takes time and the
more we fast and pray, the more we see change
happen and gain insights as we see God work
in our lives and in the lives of people we pray
for. Fasting can bring to light the motives of a
person's heart. We can ask God to reveal to us
what we need to see and what needs to be
prayed for the strongholds to break. With
prayer and fasting, truth can be brought to
light as the darkness is dispelled. Fasting and
prayer can expose the enemy's lies and deception. We can then pray to break the hold the
enemy has had over us or our loved ones and
others we feel led to pray for. The struggles and
problems we face may seem to get worse before
they get better because we are in a battle. God
is working and moving, but so is Satan. Satan
will try to attack because he is angry when we
come up against him. We can bind up Satan's
attacks and ask God for the strength to keep
praying and fighting the battle, not allowing
doubt and discouragement to enter in. We can
pray the blood of Jesus over us and over our
loved ones. Praying the blood of Jesus is like a
covering so no harm can come over us or over
anyone else we're praying for. It is also wise to
put our armor on (Eph. 6:13-17) whenever we
are doing anything for God. When we pray to

put on the full armor of God, the belt of truth, the breastplate of righteousness, our feet fitted with readiness, the shield of faith, the helmet of salvation and the sword of the Spirit, we have protection against the enemy. Nothing and no one can thwart God's will or plans (Job 42:2), but we need to do our part and fast and pray for the breakthroughs to come. No problem is too big or impossible for God to breakthrough (Luke 1:37). We will have a peace and knowing in our hearts as we put our faith and trust in God and keep praying. As we seek God and 7is Kingdom, we will see change take place and see the miracles God wants to bless us with.

We give more of ourselves to God as we fast and pray. It is being emptied of self as we look to God for guidance and direction as we pray for 7is will to be done. We die to self more each time we fast, because we are focusing on what God wants instead of on our own desires or agendas. When we're willing to be emptied of self, it's then that God can do a deep cleansing and healing work in us freeing us from strongholds and mindsets that can be blocking what God wants to do. We have to be emptied of self to be filled completely with God's love and 7is Spirit, so we can become more like Jesus. When we spend time alone with God, 7e does a transformation work in us that forever changes us. We become more submissive and yielding to 7is 7oly Spirit that enables us to see what God's will is as 7e gives us the ability and strength to do what 7e calls us to do. As we continue to fast and pray, we will see strongholds shatter, experience peace and contentment in God, find fulfillment and the abundant life God wants us to have as we watch His plan and purpose unfold.

Chapter 12

Tools the Enemy Uses to Keep Us From God's Blessings

Recognizing the tools the enemy uses gives us a better understanding of how the enemy works. Satan's main goal or objective is to keep us out of the will of the Father. Satan is the father of lies and two of the primary tools Satan uses to keep us from God's blessings are lies and deception. He lies to us about God to keep us from wanting to seek and know Him. When God made the earth and everything in it, it was perfect. God made man in His image (Gen. 1:2H) and gave him free will and dominion over the earth (Gen. 1:2J). Man was manipulated and deceived in the Garden of Eden and so began the downfall of man. Not only were there sickness, suffering and disease, but man had to work to survive. He had forfeited his right to rule and Satan became the god of this world by default. As long as man continues to be influenced, manipulated and deceived by the god of this world, suffering and unfairness will continue. Asking Jesus to come into our hearts changes our thinking and perspective. As we gain wisdom and knowledge from God, He helps us to see what we can do to bring about change.

Unless we are following God, it is difficult to know and be in His will. Satan will try to deceive and manipulate us into doing what he wants instead of what God wants. We might believe we are in God's will, unaware that we are being influenced or under Satan's deception. Something or someone can come into our lives and we feel blessed believing it is of God only to find ourselves with Satan's counterfeit instead of the real thing. We can buy into the lie we are free when we go our own way seeking to fill our own needs instead of looking to God to meet them. When we're not walking with God and living in His truth, we're rebelling against Him. Rebellion started as disobedience towards God when Adam and Eve ate of the fruit of the tree of the knowledge of good and evil in Genesis 3:6. Adam and Eve bought into the lie that they could be like God, knowing everything. The lie caused deception, but also doubt in their minds that God was trying to keep something from them. Satan likes to lie to us about God, putting fear and doubt in our minds and distorting God's truth. God wants to give good gifts to His children, but like any good parent, He also wants to protect us. We step out of God's protective covering by not being obedient to God and following Him and His ways. Rebellion is a controlling, prideful, deceptive spirit that can cause changes in our attitude and behavior. It is one of the major tools Satan uses to keep us from God's blessings. If there is pride or rebellion in our hearts we will resist the Holy Spirit and won't be able to experience the fullness of God's love and all He has for us.

Rebellion can lead us to seek guidance from other means instead of looking to God for wisdom. God gives us wisdom when we ask for it (James 1:5) and understanding comes as we grow in our knowledge of God. Seeking it through other means opens us up to deception. God gives us this warning in 1 Samuel:

Rebellion is like the sin of divination and arrogance like the evil of idolatry.
1 Sam. 15:23

Seeking knowledge through fortunetellers is practicing divination and opens us up to the spirits of darkness causing us to rebel against God. Rebellion is a stubborn controlling spirit and a root cause of sin. It is hard to break because Satan doesn't want to give up the control he has over God's children. Man's agenda and rebellious spirits hinder being able to do things God's way (Matt. 15:6,J,9). The prideful, rebellious spirits need to be broken for us to have a submissive spirit towards God's Holy Spirit. If Satan can keep us rebelling and being disobedient to God, he can keep us out of the will of the Father and the blessings God has for us.

Fear can be an underlying cause of rebellion and we may find ourselves in a situation or a relationship feeling trapped, believing the lie there's no way out. Satan will reinforce the lie with guilt or shame leading us to believe we aren't worthy of anything better. Feelings of inadequacy, unworthiness or oppression can come over us, leaving us in a state of weakness.

There can be a fear of being alone or being rejected keeping us stuck and blinding us from seeing a solution or having the courage to make changes. Satan wants to keep us trapped filling us with doubts causing feelings of hopelessness or discouragement, so we settle for something less than what God has intended for us. We don't have to believe Satan's lies that there's no way out or that we deserve to stay where we are. God is a God of hope. He wants us to have good things and will always make a way of escape (1 Cor: 10:13). We can bind up the lie we're stuck with no way out or that we're not deserving of anything better. Whenever we bind anything up, we always have to remember to bind it up in Jesus Name. It is the power of Jesus that breaks the bondage and sets us free.

The enemy will use our hurts to cause us to harden our hearts, numb our feelings and put fear in us of getting close to others. When we've been hurt we can become bitter and close ourselves off to God. Hebrew warns us of the danger of letting bitterness take root.

> *See to it that no one*
> *misses the grace of God*
> *and that no bitter root grows*
> *up to cause trouble and*
> *defile many.*
> *Hebrews 12:15*

The root of bitterness can defile a person causing a corrupt and perverse spirit to rise up in them. When a person allows bitterness to take root, they can become unhappy and dissatisfied with their lives becoming jealous of someone else and what they have. They can fall prey to the deception of the enemy when they haven't let go of the hurt and anger that has caused them to become bitter. When a person is operating under a bitter and jealous spirit, it may cause them to lie and deceive others, manipulating and using them for their own selfish means. They deceive and hurt themselves when they set out to hurt others. Self-respect, integrity and trust can be lost when lies are exposed. The thief comes to steal, kill and destroy (John 10:10). It is Satan at work behind the corrupt, deceptive and perverse spirits. God can root out these spirits when we bind them up in Jesus Name, setting a person free from bondage and out from under the deception of the enemy.

We let Satan gain a foothold when we're caught up in sin putting us in bondage to shame, guilt or fear that can lead into denial and distort our thinking. Denial represses feelings and emotions that we don't know how to deal with or are too painful for us to bear. When we're in denial we open ourselves up to lying spirits, being unwilling to face the truth. Denial is a defense mechanism, a protective wall we put up around ourselves to shield us from the truth we can't face and becomes a stronghold when we stay hiding behind it. It's a shield that keeps a person from feeling hurt and pain or allowing repressed memories to surface so they can be dealt with and resolved. The problem remains and there is no growth of change. We can't walk in the freedom of Christ when we're in denial and not willing to deal with our issues. Denial can create doubt in our minds causing confusion, conflict, turmoil, unbelief and being double-minded wavering back and forth with indecision. The enemy wants us to stay in confusion and turmoil so we can't see solutions to our problems. The walls we put up blocks us from seeing what God may be trying to reveal to us. When we bind up the turmoil, confusion, doubt and unbelief in Jesus Name, it has to leave. When the walls and defenses are down, it softens our hearts and we become open to the Lord. When the lies are exposed, it breaks the hold it has over us and truth can be revealed. Whatever emotions and feelings we have buried will come up to the surface. Releasing them to God sets us free. If the enemy tries to come in, we will have the strength to resist him. Knowing God's Word and His truth will help us to be able to distinguish the difference between God's truth and the lies the enemy uses to cause confusion and doubt in our minds. We can ask God to help us to focus on Him and to show us what needs to be prayed for us to be set free. We can intercede and pray on behalf of others and bind up any strongholds they maybe under to see them set free from the enemy.

Our enemy is at work to try to sear our consciences to the things of God. Compromising our values can desensitize us to sin, letting the enemy gain more ground in our lives. It can weaken our faith and relationship with God. The more we allow things in that aren't of God, the more power we give Satan that can weaken our moral values. It allows Satan to enter in with thoughts to torment us by reminding us of our failures. When our failures or things we've done that we're not proud of come back to torment us, they are still having control over us. It can cause feelings of inferiority and low self worth. Satan will use that against us causing us to feel worse about ourselves. He wants to bring us down by reminding us of our shortcomings and torments us with things we've done wrong. God is a forgiving God. He wants to encourage us and to be free from all condemnation and the lies of the enemy. There is no condemnation for those who are in Christ Jesus (Rom. J:1). He gives grace and mercy and forgiveness when we fall short of His glory (Rom. 3:23). God wants us to live right because it brings blessings and keeps us free from the enemy and from harm. God can break us free from wrong beliefs, distorted thinking and help us to let go of our failures. Our self-confidence and self worth grows as we release our burdens to God and we become stronger in the Lord. Satan does not have power over God's children. When we give our lives to Christ, we have the power and authority to drive out the devil and his scheming ways. It is up to us to exercise God's power and not believe the lies of the enemy that we are helpless victims. It doesn't mean that we are to be complacent and ignore the fact that he is real and exists and will try to attack when we feel weak. There will be times we have to do battle in the spiritual realm through fasting and prayer to win the Victory for our loved ones and ourselves. God wants us to be content in Him and with what we have, but He has so much more for us. We can put our confidence, trust and faith in the Lord, because we have the assurance that He is working for our good (Rom. J:2J).

Jesus often spoke through parables to help us gain wisdom and knowledge. In Matt. 13, Jesus gives examples in the parable of the sower. A farmer was sowing seed and some fell along the path. The seed is the Word of God planted in one's heart. When God's Word was not understood, the evil one quickly snatches it away. The seed that fell on a rocky surface without much soil, withered quickly because it had no root. When we're not rooted in the Word of God and trouble comes, we won't have enough faith to stand up under persecution. It makes us weaker, causing us to fall more easily into sin. The seed that fell among thorns becomes unfruitful even after hearing the Word, because of the worries of this life and the deceitfulness of wealth. When our focus is on God, we are not so prone to worry about our circumstances or money. When we become too focused on wealth, we can miss out on what God has planned for us. God knows we need money to live, food to eat and clothes to wear (Matt. 6:31-32). Jesus said, "but seek first His kingdom and His righteousness and all these things will be given to you" (Matt. 6:33). We don't need to worry or fear that God won't take care of us because He has promised in His Word He will. The seed that falls on good soil produces a crop many times what was sown. It is hearing God's Word and understanding it. We are more likely to lean on God and trust in

Him when we know and understand His Word. In Matt. 13:15, Jesus explains that many who have hardened their hearts can hardly hear and have closed their eyes. It is because of their hardened hearts they don't see or understand. God wants us to open our hearts so we will understand His Word and be able to stand against the enemy.

Satan is a master at deception and will use our weaknesses and whatever means he can to take us further away from our walk with God and living for Him. We are in a constant battle in our minds and with our emotions. There can be deep things God needs to root out of us that are blocking and standing in the way of God's will and what He wants to bring into our lives. When we are struggling with issues or fears, we can ask God to help us to let go, so we can be free of them. Having an understanding of the spiritual realm helps us to see how strongholds can be broken in our hearts and minds. God has given us the power to break Satan's hold over us through the blood of Jesus. It is God working through us and not under our own power. We don't have any power outside of Jesus. We are under deception if we believe that. We need to pray for fortitude of mind to make us stronger in the Lord, to break free from any defeatist attitudes, victim mentality or negativity. We need strength in God to win the battle. When we are freed from the bondage to sin, we can have Victory over our lives. God is a loving God and didn't come to condemn us, but to set us free from the enemy. He wants to tear down the strongholds in our minds and hearts, so we can live free in Him. We can bind up whatever is keeping us bound in Jesus Name. We need to be diligent and have the desire and determination to keep the freedom we've gained and guard our hearts against the enemy of our souls.

It can feel like a battle as Satan tries to keep us bound and God is at work to set us free. In facing trials, we find out how much we need God and His strength and divine intervention to win the battles we face. Satan tries to make us believe we are weak if we lean on God so he can have the advantage over us. When we acknowledge our weaknesses and give them over to God, He can put His strength in us. We fight against Satan and the principalities of darkness in God's strength and through the power of prayer. It makes us strong when we are operating and leaning on God's strength and not our own, giving us Victory over the powers of darkness and in our situations. Letting pride, rebellion or disobedience get in the way, blinds us to God's truth and leaves us open to deception. Letting go allows us to see through the deception, putting our strength and trust in God to win the battle. We have to bind up wanting to do things our way instead of God's way and any pride, rebellion or disobedience that may be at work in us to gain Victory.

When we've been under Satan's oppression, power or influence through our weaknesses or addictions and we overcome them, we come out stronger. God uses people that have come through addictions, fears or whatever the enemy has used to keep them bound to help others to recognize the tactics of the enemy and how to break free. Jesus gave 7is life so we could be saved and be reunited with the Father, but 7e also gave us power and authority over the enemy to put him under our feet. We give Satan more power then he really has by believing his lies and letting him have control. 7e will use any underhanded trick, lie, deception, fear or any weaknesses we have to try to keep us from God's blessings. 7e likes to convince us he has more power by manipulating and twisting the truth to suit his own purposes causing us to doubt God. If he can keep us under his influence instead of us using the power and authority we rightfully have through Christ, Satan can immobilize Christians from doing the will of the Father. Standing on God's Word and praying against the enemy helps us to resist his ploys and defeat him. We have to exercise our authority in Christ. When we don't back down, we become conquers and gain Victory over our situations and our lives. If we're living right in Christ, we will recognize the enemy's tactics and we won't leave ourselves open to deception. It doesn't mean we won't be attacked, only that we will have the tools and knowledge to know how to fight against them. When we're under the blood of Jesus and walking with God, we will be protected.

We can use the authority we have in Jesus to come against Satan's attacks, whether there is fear, oppression, discouragement or physical attacks on our body. When we rise above and conquer the oppressive and depressive spirits, we will have hope and confidence and strength to follow God and to do His will. We need to realize the awesome power of God and have the faith belief and knowledge that Satan is a defeated foe. Satan can blind us to the truth, but we don't need to give in to the lies and feelings of defeat. We need to rise up in faith belief to come against the wiles of the enemy and chose the Victory in Jesus that He has won for us and wants to give us. Satan will try to keep us down, but that's when we need to call on God to fight for us. God wants us to be free. Learning to trust God gives us the faith that He will see us through anything we are faced with. When we pray, we fight against the enemy in the spiritual realm where God can move and make changes in our lives and in the lives of people we pray for. When we are truly rooted in God's Word, we will believe and know that we have the Victory in Jesus.

Chapter 13

Fear and Unbelief: Major Stumbling Blocks

Asking Jesus to come into our hearts and seeing the change it's made in us, makes it difficult to see why we can still struggle with fear and unbelief. Fear and unbelief are major stumbling blocks and a prime area that Satan uses to try to cause doubt in our minds about God. Fear is a powerful emotion that can cause panic, worry, anxiety, doubt, shame, guilt, unworthiness and feelings of vulnerability. We can be in denial of our fears and as long as they stay hidden, we're unable to conquer them. Fear and unbelief can lead to rebellion, disobedience and doubting God's Word and His truth. When there is fear, we will feel insecure and have trouble trusting and believing God and try to do things under our own strength. It becomes a block in our relationship with God and learning to be dependant on Him. Fear can be a controlling force in our lives, especially if there's fear of losing something precious in our lives or a fear of being alone. Fear of losing, fear of failing, of being hurt again or being rejected can hinder us from stepping out in faith. Deep-seated fears can keep us trapped and out of the will of God, paralyzing us from moving forward, maturing and growing in Him. It's much easier to stay in our comfort zone and feel some sense of control instead of believing God and stepping out in faith. We may feel the need to want to control others or our circumstances as a way to feel in control. We may find it difficult to believe how God has complete control and be unable to see how He can change our circumstances or our lives.

Fear and unbelief can block us from seeing, believing and accepting the truth. There can be lies we believe that are buried in our subconscious mind and our fears and unbelief can hinder us from seeing what the lies are. The fear we've repressed and buried has to be uprooted and come to the surface to expose the lies. Believing lies can be easier then believing and facing the truth if we're not ready to face it. We can allow the truth to become twisted and distorted in our minds if facing the truth causes fear in us. There can be a fear of the unknown, of growing up, of making changes to become what God has designed for us to be or to fulfill what He is calling us to do. Rooting out the fear and unbelief is critical in our walk with God and taking the step of faith to follow Him and to be in His will. If we don't break free from our fears, it holds us back from experiencing all that God has to offer us. If we've been exposed to false teaching, it can become a block in our hearts and minds affecting our relationship with Christ. In believing the false teaching, we can experience confusion and doubt in our minds leading to unbelief or fear and be uncertain of God's love for us. With so many different religions, legalistic thinking or man's own agenda, God's truth can get distorted in our minds. It can hinder our ability to learn what God wants to teach us causing our faith to be weak. The false teaching needs to be bound up in the Name of Jesus. We can ask God to root out the seeds of where it came from, releasing us from bondage and freeing us to believe and see the truth. Letting go of fear, unbelief, lies and false teaching allows God to do an inner healing work in us setting us free.

Fear of failure is another area that can keep us from moving forward in God. Experiencing failure can be difficult to work through if it has shattered our confidence. When we've failed in jobs or relationships, it maybe that it wasn't what God had intended for us. If we can look upon our failures and mistakes as learning tools, they will no longer have a hold on us. Instead of punishing or blaming ourselves for mistakes we've made, we can ask God to turn them around for His good and glory. We may be able to help others gain insights from what we've learned to help them turn their lives around when they've faced failure. Letting go of our failures helps us to learn to take risks again. Fear can hinder us from being able to let go. As long as we hang onto the fear, we'll find it hard to let go. The more we learn to let go, the more we find our trust and faith in God grows. He made us and He has the power to make things happen. We may find our desires and dreams change as God works in our hearts. He has given us talents and abilities and wants us to realize our full potential. To see the life God has purposed and designed for us, we need a humble and submissive heart and be willing to let God show us what He wants for us. If we trust and believe God and are open to His leading and guidance, we will be where we need to be, doing what He has purposed for us to do. We gain confidence as we learn to step out in faith that God will lead and guide us in the right direction.

Unbelief can be a root cause of our fears, of not trusting God, doubting and being double-minded. There are lying and deceptive spirits at work behind fear and unbelief. When we have fear, we struggle to trust and believe God and instead believe the lies of the enemy, causing more doubt, fear and uncertainty in our lives. Feelings of unworthiness and feeling undeserving can have its roots in fear and unbelief. We can have a fear of not measuring up or a fear of rejection leading to self-doubt and unbelief. If we don't feel worthy we may reject what God has for us for fear we don't deserve it or are good enough. We may believe we're not worthy of love if we have suffered from rejection and hurt and won't let anyone get too close. It is often painful experiences we've gone through that has shaken our security and trust causing us to be fearful of getting too close and opening up to others. We find ways to distance ourselves and push other people away when we become uncomfortable with too much closeness. We may chose partners that are emotionally distance because of our fear of getting too close and stay in unhealthy relationships because of our fear of being alone. We may find ourselves unhappy, resentful and angry for not having the courage and strength to overcome our fears and leave an unhealthy situation. The fear can cause us to have unbelief that God wants and has something better for us. Satan will use our fear of being hurt again to hide from true love, blinding us to our needs and from opening ourselves up to God and others. God can deliver us from our fears of being hurt and help us to learn to trust again. We can overcome our fears by turning to God and asking Him to help us to let go of our fears and unbelief.

We live fragmented lives when we are bound emotionally and spiritually to fear and unbelief and other things that stand in the way of doing God's will. We can't effectively do the will of the Father when we're filled with fear or have unbelief. Fears can be stubborn because they are controlling spirits that can hinder and block us from doing God's will. We need to break the hold Satan has had over us or we will fall prey to his attacks and be ineffective for Christ. To be used by God and be effective, He has to root out the lying and deceptive spirits, the lies we believe and anything else that could be causing fear and unbelief. Breaking strongholds loosens the hold they have over us, but God still needs to get to the root cause. There can be deep underlying root causes of why we struggle with fear and unbelief. When we have suffered through many disappointments, it can shatter our faith and cause us to struggle to believe God when He has given us a promise or a revelation of things to come. Satan wants to put doubt in our minds of God not coming through for us. Doubt causes us to give up hope that can lead to depressed feelings, discouragement, hopelessness and negative thinking. It causes our faith to be weak and hinders our walk with God. Satan wants to take our hope away, so we settle on a life less worthwhile, instead of waiting on God and believing Him that He will make good on His promises. We know God's Word is true, but can still find ourselves fighting with doubts without realizing why. When there are underlying root causes, it can stem from lies we believe. When God begins a deep work in us to root out the problems areas, lies we believe can surface from our subconscious mind into our awareness and be exposed to the light of His truth. The underlying causes of our fear and unbelief could have come from being passed on through the generations and things we've believed growing up. When we bind up the transference of the generational spirit of fear and unbelief and the lying and deceptive spirits in the Name of Jesus and ask God to root out the seeds and cause of them, He will do a deep work in us cleansing us and healing us, freeing us from all our fears and unbelief. God will fill us with His perfect love that casts out all fear (1 John 4:1J). Even when God has rooted out our fears, they can surface again when we are asked to do something that scares us. We can let it rule us or make that choice to say yes to God and step out in faith conquering our fears to have Victory in Christ. God wants to take us past our fears, doubts and unbelief not only for us to live abundant lives, but to enable us to follow Him and to do His will. The key to getting rid of fear and unbelief is to turn our focus to

God. When we are able to look to God and take our eyes off our circumstances, it opens up our mind to see solutions and gives us hope. When Peter kept his focus on Jesus, he walked on water (Matt. 14:2J,29). As soon as he took his eyes off of Jesus and saw the wind, he became afraid and cried out to the Lord as he began to sink (Matt. 14:30). Jesus reached out 7is hand to catch him, then asked him why he had such little faith and doubted (Matt. 14:31). In Exodus 3:10, God calls Moses to bring the Israelites out of Egypt. Moses said, "Who am I that I should go to Pharaoh and bring the Israelites out of Egypt?" 7e could not see how he could accomplish what God wanted him to do. 7e was looking at the natural and not at what God could do through him. 7ebrews 3:7-19 gives an account of how Moses led the Israelites out of Egypt, but because of their unbelief, they wandered in the desert for 40 years. Their hearts were always going astray because they did not know God's ways. Their unbelieving hearts turned away from the living God. The Israelites were not able to enter God's rest because of their unbelief. When we look to ourselves, our thinking is limited. Putting our focus on God, we'll go in God's strength and authority and not our own. That truth has to sink into our spirits to give us the determination in our hearts and minds to believe that whatever God asks of us, 7e will give us the ability to accomplish it.

Although there is a battle going on in our minds, what is in our hearts can affect our thinking. In Genesis, we read that after the fall of man, men's hearts had turned away from

God. Gen. 6:5 states, "The Lord saw how great man's wickedness on the earth had become, and that every inclination of the thoughts of his heart was only evil all the time." Turning away from God will cause us to have a heart of unbelief and we will constantly struggle with doubts and believing God loves us or will come through for us. The root cause of having fear and unbelief is the rebellion that lives in our hearts. Rebellion causes us to doubt God, leading to unbelief and fear. When we don't believe, we won't be obedient to God. When Adam and Eve sinned against God in the Garden of Eden, unbelief and rebellion took root in their hearts. They allowed Satan to deceive them putting doubt in their hearts and minds about God. To root out the seeds and cause of our unbelief, we have to root out the rebellion in our hearts. God can change our hearts of unbelief to a heart of belief and teach us how to put our trust and faith in Him. It's so vital for believing God to come through for us, to meet our needs and to have healing. We can pray for God to do a spiritual cleansing in our hearts and minds to wash away the rebellion and our unbelief and fear. When we pray for God to cleanse our spiritual eyes, it opens our eyes to see the truth and praying to cleanse our spiritual ears opens our ears to hear the truth and the voice of God. When our hearts are changed, the way we think will change. It opens our eyes to see things clearer and we have more discernment making us more sensitive to the things of God. Cleansing our hearts and minds not only removes the fear, it makes us spiritually stronger. When a heart of unbelief is changed to a heart of believing God, we will begin to see our lives changed from a mundane existence to a life filled with promise and fulfillment.

Fear can cause us to be disobedient to God and run from what He is calling us to do. We can rationalize, thinking and believing we aren't being disobedient to God, when in reality we may not be willing to listen to Him. The root and underlying cause of much of our struggle with obedience to God has to do with fear and unbelief. We need the fear of the Lord in us (Proverbs 1:7). The fear of the Lord is a reverence and awe of God, not the kind that makes us run the other way. Having the fear of the Lord in us causes us to want to be obedient to Him. We will know He wants what is best for us and that we can trust Him. When we don't have a fear and reverence for the Lord, we tend to be rebellious and want to do things our own way. When there is fear, Satan can twist things in our minds and cause us to believe we are in God's will when we're not. We can put walls up to hide behind so we don't have to deal with reality and the truth that we're being disobedience and rebelling against God. When there are walls up, it's like a veil covering our eyes and we're in spiritual darkness. God has to break down the walls, for the veil to be lifted off our eyes so we can see the truth. Satan wants us to stay in darkness and in fear because he knows fear can paralyze us from moving forward in God. Fear becomes a block to hearing and following God and knowing what His will is. God maybe prompting us to do something that causes fear in us and we unknowingly tune Him out because of the fear. We may keep going in the direction we think we should go and stubbornly forge ahead instead of listening and being obedient to God. Fear can get in the way of doing God's will because it causes us to resist God's Holy Spirit and we will feel the need to escape from His calling when we are filled with fear. Satan uses fear because he's afraid of what we as Christians could accomplish if we didn't let fear stand in the way. Fear can cause us to believe the lie we are too weak to be used by God. We only need to be willing vessels for God to be used by Him to further His Kingdom. God gives us the strength and ability to do the work He calls us to do. When we are willing to step out in faith and be a willing vessel for God, we will gain satisfaction and a feeling of accomplishment knowing we are doing something that will make a difference in other people's lives. We can miss out on the many blessings God has for us when we allow fear and unbelief to rule us.

Learning to release our fears to God and asking Him to root out the cause of them will bring healing. When we've given our hearts to God and become Born Again, we may not have completely given our lives or control over to Him. It's difficult to live a life of Victory in Christ or live completely in God's will when we want to be in control. Giving the control over to God, gives us peace and contentment. Our focus will change from self to one more centered on God. As we die to self and let go of our fears and unbelief, we will see God's plan and purpose unfold. As we step out in faith in God's strength and have learned to trust in Him, we will be able to conquer our fears. Once we obtain Victory in one area of our lives, Satan loses power over us as that weak area in us becomes stronger. We find ourselves growing and maturing more in God, as our faith and strength in Him grows making us stronger Christians. We will feel more drawn to the Lord and closer to Him and we will feel a greater desire and longing to fulfill His perfect will. It's the Holy Spirit that works in us to draw us closer to the Lord. God wants us to have a faith so great, we are willing to give our all to Him and not be afraid to become what He has destined for us to be. All we need is a willing heart and a deep desire to know and follow Him.

Chapter 14

Counterfeit Spirits
& The False Self

There can be various reasons people have a false self. It can make a person feel safe when they hide the part of themselves they're not comfortable revealing to others. A person may hide behind a false self if they have been deeply hurt and have difficulty letting others get too close. The false self is a wall one puts up to hide from their true self and is used to protect and shield them from being vulnerable to anymore hurt or pain. A person can have a false self or put on a false front if they don't believe they're good enough or fear others won't accept them for who they are. There maybe something they want to keep hidden and fear what others will think of them if the truth was revealed. Many of us live with the fear of being rejected or worry that we will be unable to live up to other's expectations.

Revealing our true selves puts us in a vulnerable position of possibly being rejected and the fear of rejection can keep us bound to a false self. We may feel like we'll never quite measure up and a false self is our protective covering or shell to protect our true selves. If we don't feel accepted for who we are, having a false self or putting on a false front could be a way for us to seek approval and acceptance in man instead of looking to God. A false front can hide our insecurities and fears and be a way to feel in control when inside we feel out of control. On the outside, it could appear like we have it altogether, but on the inside we could be struggling with insecurities, feeling inadequate and suffer with low self worth. Being rejected by others that have played a significance role in our lives or negative words spoken to us only serves to amplify our already shaken identity. We can break the fear or lie we don't measure up or that we're not good enough in Jesus Name and ask God to root out the seeds and cause of our fears and insecurities. Having God as a solid foundation and looking to Him for our self worth helps us to accept ourselves even if others don't.

To gain a better perspective and have compassion and understanding of a person's need to hide from their true selves, we have to look deeper into a person's heart. There can be deep issues a person is struggling with that has caused them to put on a false self. The part of the self that is hidden and locked away is the one that has suffered deep hurts that haven't been healed. Those wounds can be so painful, a person can be in denial, putting on a false self or false front when they are not ready to face or deal with the truth or hurt and pain in their lives. A person can be so deep in denial they are in a type of prison. Reality and truth are distorted and the falsehood they are living becomes their reality. The false self is used as a coping mechanism when a person has not learned to cope or deal with reality. It can make one feel safe, but it keeps one from facing the truth they may not be ready to deal with or can't face. Being in denial can open a person up to lying spirits. A lying spirit will work through a person to lie and deceive others, but it also causes self-deception. A person can twist the truth in their minds and believe their own lies. The lie can become so firmly cemented in their minds, they actually believe it as truth. The Lord can unravel the truth that has been twisted in a person's mind. We can pray on behalf of anyone we know that has a false self for God to break down the walls exposing those areas needed so God can bring healing and change can take place. Only when those issues are brought into a person's awareness, can the unresolved conflicts and hurt and pain surface, so it can be dealt with and healed. When a lying spirit becomes deep rooted, it's not only the lying spirits that need binding up in Jesus Name, but the power, authority, control and influence these spirits can have over the heart, mind, spirit, soul, will and emotions of the person under deception. The seeds and cause of the lying spirit taking root in a person's heart also needs to be bound up in the Name of Jesus.

Putting on a false front or having a false self can be a learned behavior. It can stem from religious spirits that can cause a distorted view of God because it operates under man's agenda instead of God's truth. Religious spirits are controlling spirits that use fear, intimidation, shame or guilt. It can cause repressed feelings and emotions when we don't feel free to express them or know how to deal with them. We may have learned to be more concerned with what other people think and are taught what we feel isn't important and deny, repress and bury our own feelings and needs. Living up to other's expectations and trying to please them causes frustration and we become people pleasers instead of looking to please God. We pretend we're happy and can even convince ourselves we are, but in doing so, we lose a part of ourselves. The longer we stay hidden behind a false self, the more we can feel lost, alone or insecure. It's not until we begin to uncover the layers that mask our true selves are we able to discover who we are and begin to live in truth and reality.

Putting on a false self or false pretenses opens the doors to counterfeit spirits. In having a false self, we lack discernment to see what is real and what's not, making us more vulnerable to counterfeit spirits. Counterfeit spirits are deceptive spirits that lie to us and often disguise themselves as angels of light (2 Cor. 11:14). They are powerful because they can gain control over us by using their power and authority and influence causing us to believe lies. Counterfeit spirits can bring people and things into our lives and we may feel happy for a time, but it's a ploy of the enemy to keep us out of God's will (2 Thess. 2:9). Counterfeit spirits can create a stronghold over us when we believe what we have is real when it's not and can lure us into a false sense of security. Satan wants us to have a false sense of security and keep us believing what we have is real to block out the truth and keep us out of God's will. We may have a heart for God and truly have the desire to follow Him and be in His will, but when we accept the counterfeit, we reject what God has for us. Counterfeit, lying deceiving spirits block out God's voice and hinder God's will being done by convincing us we're going in the direction God wants us to go in. Satan is out to deceive us and if he can make us believe we are hearing God, he can keep us going in the wrong direction and out of the will of the Father. Nothing can thwart God's plan, but it can cause delays or roadblocks that we have to pray against. God can move and break through the counterfeit spirits when we bind them up in Jesus Name. We need to cover ourselves with the blood of Jesus whenever we are binding up spirits and commanding them to leave because Satan will try to attack when we're confronting these spirits and praying against them. Praying what needs to be broken penetrates the layers of deception and walls that have been built up in the heart and mind that cover and mask the truth.

Willing to be open to God gives us discernment to help us recognize the ploys of the enemy. He brings destruction and sets his trap by steering us in the wrong direction through counterfeit spirits. He wants us to feel a false sense of peace or security to serve a purpose. Things may appear to be good for a time before they turn on us. We only have to look to the Bible and read through the tribulation when the Anti-Christ comes on the scene in (2 Thess. 2:3). He gains people's trust and lures them into a false peace. After the first three and half years of peace, everything turns and the people are then brought under the control of the beast described in Rev. 13: 5-8. We can see how our lives can parallel to warnings given in the Bible. When we have a false sense of security, our security isn't in God and we can be easily deceived and lured into a false sense of peace. It's when our safe world collapses and our false self is stripped away that we're left with the truth and reality we eventually have to face. Being stripped of our false self exposes the motives of our hearts to reveal the darkness that lives there and our need to be real and honest with ourselves. God wants us to live in reality and His truth. We have to be open to God and honest with ourselves to see the truth and to be willing to deal with reality. God doesn't want us living with a false self, not only because we deceive ourselves, but it also keeps us from seeing the truth and from living the life God has planned for us. The counterfeit lying spirits gives us a false sense of self and creates fear, doubt and unbelief in our minds. It can become deep rooted and cause us to struggle with believing and trusting God. When we don't have our faith belief in God, we have no anchor for our security and become fearful. A lying spirit can convince us we're no good. If we don't feel worthy we won't believe God to give us something good and we will reject it when God tries to bring it into our lives. God can be knocking on the doors of our hearts, but when there's too much darkness standing in the way, we won't let Him in. God wants to get to the deep roots to break through the false pretenses and the facades and walls we put up to hide behind to bring healing and set us free. It's the work of the Holy Spirit in us that is able to do a complete healing work changing us. God wants to give us His true peace and to heal us, cleansing us and making us whole and complete in Him. God desires for us to live an abundant life that can only come by living in truth and reality.

Chapter 15

Breaking Generational Bondages

As imperfect human beings living in a fallen world, the outcome has created dysfunction in families and generational bondages. Our parents may have been encouraging, caring, loving parents doing the best they can, making it difficult to understand why we struggle in some areas of our lives. Physical problems, feelings of inadequacy, loneliness, failure or disappointments as well as other negative feelings and learned patterns all can be transferred and passed on through the generations. Depression, rejection or feelings of unworthiness are some other common problem areas we can find difficult to overcome. Without emotional and inner healing, we'll continue to battle against these negative feelings and emotions. God can help us to overcome any problem areas we're battling with by bringing them into our awareness and as we release them to God, He can bring healing. We can pray for healing for our parents and anyone else we know of that is hurting and in need of God's healing touch.

In the world in which we live, we can be constantly bombarded with negative messages either through the media or other experiences we encounter as we go through life's journey.

The world often measures us not by who we are, but by what we do or how much money we make. The problem that rises up from measuring ourselves by these standards and trying to live up to them brings on the very feelings or emotions that we are trying to break free of. We can experience feelings of inadequacy, shame or guilt that can cause depression, loneliness, emptiness and feelings of unworthiness. If we suffer from inadequacy, we will feel that somehow we don't quite measure up and will doubt God's love for us. Experiencing any of these types of feelings can affect our relationship with God and with others. If we're feeling unworthy, we will struggle with believing we will have what we want or need or that God loves us enough to bring us what we need. Any area that we struggle with and is deep-rooted will often have their roots in generational bondages that have been transferred and projected onto us. The bondages need to be broken and everything rooted up and out of us to be free of them so healing can take place.

Depression can be transferred from generation to generation and become a crippling bondage because it can have such a devastating effect on our lives. It is not uncommon for depression to be deep rooted when it has been passed down through many generations. Depression that has been passed down through the generations is a spiritual bondage that can be broken by binding it up in Jesus Name. If the depression or oppressed feelings don't leave after binding them up, we can ask God to get to the root and bring to mind whatever the underlying issues are that are causing the depressed feelings to linger. When it's deep rooted, there can be feelings that are buried that need to surface for us to break completely free of the spiritual depression or oppression we are under. Once God brings things to our mind, we can release them to 7im. It's letting go of them that brings healing.

There can be other reasons for suffering with depression that may not have been passed down onto us. There maybe medical reasons that need to be treated. If we have suffered the loss of a loved one, we need time to grieve and work through the grief to get passed the depressed feelings. The rejection, emptiness and loneliness we go through from loss are not easily overcome. We may not feel loved or valued for who we are that can cause feelings of depression. It is typical to isolate ourselves or withdraw from others when we feel depressed. Negative thinking patterns can be a learned behavior that can fuel our feelings of depression and hinder our ability to cope with life's problems. Going through disappointments or experiencing job loss can cause discouragement and the belief our lives will never change. It can become a life long struggle that only through God's love and breaking through strongholds can we see light at the end of the tunnel. God's 7oly Spirit (John 14:26,27) is our counselor and comforter and is here for us and wants to help us work through our feelings of grief and despair to bring healing. If we need to talk to someone to help us work through our grief, God can lead and guide us to the right person. God helps us to renew our minds and change our thinking as He breaks us free from depression.

Fears can be passed down through the generations, but they can also come out of our own experiences. Often times when we struggle with fear, we find ourselves in the very situations that make us fearful. We can have a fear of rejection, of being alone or a fear of not being accepted for who we are. We have a built in need to be accepted and when we aren't it creates a void causing us to feel empty and alone. The generational bondage of fear of being rejected can cause insecurities or fear of failure that will surface when we've been rejected or hurt. Rejection can cause feeling of loneliness and unworthiness and believing we're not good enough. If we use avoidance patterns as a defense mechanism to avoid dealing with our fears, we will never be free of them. We have to be willing to face our fears and let them surface so God can help us be free of them. The roots and seeds of rejection and fear need to be rooted out of us so we will feel worthy and loved. When they are rooted out and we are healed from them, we will be able to feel God's love and know He loves us. We can bind up any and all these feelings and emotions that we are struggling with in the Name of Jesus and ask God to root out the seeds and cause of them. Only God can deliver us from the bondages and burdens we have been carrying that have been passed down onto us. If we aren't delivered from them, we will unknowingly and unintentionally pass them down onto our children and they will struggle in the same areas and will repeat the same patterns in their lives.

Satan likes to blind us to our need for God and feeds us lies that can be passed down through the generations. Prejudices, anger, hatred, guilt or shame to name a few, can be passed on and projected onto us. We can believe lies that we may not be aware of. They need to be brought to light through prayer and asking God to expose the lies and to break the stronghold they've had over us. They can stem from conditioning, from our childhood or from things we have been taught and believed as truth. Wrong beliefs will continue to be passed on through the generations until the cycle and pattern is broken. We cannot break a cycle or pattern until the lies we've believed have been exposed. Once they are brought into our awareness, they lose their power over us. As God exposes the lies, we can bind up them up and ask God to root them out and heal us from the damage they've caused. When we ask God to root out the lies we've believed, memories and things we have experienced will come up to the surface. If we have bound them up, but still find ourselves walking in a way that is stopping us from moving forward or we keep experiencing setbacks in our lives, we may need to dig deeper to find root causes that are still keeping us bound. Once a lie has been exposed, we may discover there are deeper issues and more lies that have to be revealed and dealt with to be free and experience complete healing.

Many learned behaviors are passed down through the generations. Alcoholism, substance abuse or being workaholics are learned behavior patterns that can be used as a coping mechanism if we were not taught healthier ways of dealing with issues. Destructive behavior patterns can lead into abusive relationships, drinking or drugs if we have not learned better ways of coping with life. We can use these means of coping to cover up feelings and emotions that we don't always know how to deal with. Feelings of loneliness, depression or rejection can be so strong we long to cover up these feelings and emotions with substances that numb our feelings. Repressing our feelings and emotions to avoid dealing with them are unhealthy learned behavior patterns that don't resolve our problems. Feelings don't go away by repressing them. They remain buried, but cause problems in our lives. Events and people can trigger them and cause uncomfortable feelings in us and we don't always know why. It can affect how we view life and how we deal with relationships and can contribute to the cause of many relationship difficulties. We may be totally unaware of what is causing problems until situations arise that trigger negative feelings and emotions in us and we are forced to deal with our issues. Deep-rooted feelings of loneliness and emptiness can be caused by rejection, but they can also stem from the fall of man and our separation from God. The void from separation can only be filled with the love of the Father. Without God in our lives and being otherwise unable to cope with our problems, we tend to follow the same patterns we've learned that have been passed down onto us.

God wants us to learn new ways of coping and resolving our problems and to break destructive thoughts and patterns in our lives. The unhealthy means we may have used before that has led to addictions or avoidance patterns need to be broken. God can help us through the process to break free from addictions, old habits and patterns so we can find better ways of dealing with our problems. He can then show us how to change old patterns and behaviors into healthier ones. We have to find healthier ways to learn to deal with our feelings and emotions if we are to overcome the negative behavior patterns. Letting go and giving everything over to God can be our turning point. It is admitting we can't do it on our own and that we need God. As we submit our wills to God, listening to Him and allowing Him to help us make the necessary changes, we can break free from our old behavior patterns. God can lead us down the road to recovery restoring us, making us whole in Him, renewing our thinking and minds through Christ. God will teach us a new way of coping and dealing with problems making us stronger.

We need to seek God's strength, wisdom and guidance if we are to see breakthroughs. When things are so deep rooted, they can take time to surface and it can be hard for us to let go. Patterns and habits passed on down through the generations have to be broken. It can takes years to break through deep rooted ones as many layers have to come off to get to the core root of the old patterns and habits to break free of them. If our parents are worriers and full of fear we will find ourselves constantly fighting against those same traits passed onto us. They become embedded in our minds and have to be broken for our minds to be renewed in Christ. We need God's supernatural intervention to break us free, but we have to be willing and submissive to His leading and allow Him to free us.

> *"I am the vine, and my*
> *Father is the gardener. He*
> *cuts off every branch in me*
> *that bears no fruit, while every*
> *branch that does bear fruit*
> *he prunes so that it will be*
> *even more fruitful."*
> *John 15:1,2*

We can think of ourselves like a big oak tree. God breaks off branches that don't bear good fruit. The branches can be strongholds preventing us from being all we can be and receiving what God has for us. As the tree is big and the roots go down deep underneath the soil, it is like that with us. There can be a number of areas in us that need healing or we need to be freed from. Each layer has to come off and as it does, more light shines through. We will have a sense of worthiness and a knowing we are loved when God takes us through a healing process and roots out negative feelings and what has caused them. As repressed feelings and emotions surface and are healed, another layer comes off and we are drawn closer to God.

We can pray and ask God to reverse the damaging effects from negative experiences and feelings or words spoken to us. Hurtful words spoken to us or over us can seep down deep into our subconscious minds, hearts and spirits. It can leave damaging effects and cause low self worth and feelings of unworthiness. It can leave us feeling weak and wounded with a lack of confidence in ourselves and our abilities. Some things can stay rooted in our minds causing us to have victim like thinking and feeling defeated. Binding them up and asking God to root these things out of us, breaks the stronghold over us, but reversing them has a profound effect on our healing. We can learn to overcome and defeat the negative messages by asking God to reverse the damaging effects they have had on us. When God reverses the damage negative words have caused, it causes our thinking to change. It brings a change in our attitude and how we look at things. When the damaging effects are reversed, it brings healing. God can go deeper, penetrating into our hearts, minds and souls to heal the hurt and pain of the damage that has been done to us through someone's actions or thoughtless words. Some scars can be very deep rooted and will leave a void when God roots them out and leave us feeling vulnerable and exposed. It's important to ask God to fill us with His love and protection over us as things are rooted out of us so nothing else can enter in. God wants to fill the void with His love and give us healing, making us whole and complete in Him. As we are freed from bondage we become more confident, spiritually aware, and more in tune with God. God can reverse the damaging effects of the rejection and hurt we've been through and help us to know and feel God's love and acceptance. We can turn the rejection we've gone through into a knowing that we are accepted and loved by God. We can pray to reverse the damage our fears have caused us and turn it into faith. God will root out the seeds and cause of the hurt, rejection and fear in our hearts and fill us with His love. We will feel more secure in the Lord and it will increase our faith and trust in Him.

We can renew our minds through God's help and reading the Bible to help keep us on the right track. Changing our thinking brings us into a greater awareness and understanding. As our minds are renewed it changes our attitudes and leads to a change of heart. If our patterns and thinking don't change, we can't expect our lives to. God wants to get to the root of our problems. He doesn't just cover them up, but cleanses and frees us from them. When we've been set free, it can be easy to fall back into old patterns and behaviors if we're not careful and lose the freedom God gave us. It is our responsibility to stay free and learn to walk in the freedom Christ bought for us. If God has freed us from addictions or any other form of bondage we need to stay away from it. We deceive ourselves to think because Christ freed us we can dabble in it again. We will only put ourselves in bondage to it again and have to go through the whole process again. We can't live abundant lives if we are stuck in old patterns and old ways of thinking. We can be set free through Christ, but it's our choice to stay free. We need to be free from the generational bondages from our past to be able to step out in faith belief to believe God for His promises and feel and know that we are truly loved and valued by God. God will pour out His Spirit onto His children, breaking through strongholds and setting us free from generational bondages. When we are freed, God can fill us with His love, strength and courage enabling us to do what we are meant to do and live our lives free in Christ.

Chapter 16

Breaking the Chains of Bondage

We can all be blinded and deceived by the enemy. To walk in Christ's freedom we need to be free from sin and the bondage it puts us in. One of the main causes of the breakdown of our society and being blinded by sin is not having the fear of the Lord in us. 7aving fear and reverence for the Lord is having great respect for God and a desire to live for 7im. It's having the knowing in our hearts and minds that God knows what is best for us and wants to give us good things and keep us from harm. God made a way for us to be truly free in 7im when Jesus died for our sins (1 John 4:9,10). When we accept Jesus into our hearts (John 3:16), we become Born Again and followers of Christ. The 7oly Spirit works in us to lead and guide us into righteous living. We all fall short of the glory of God (Rom. 3:23) but when we fail, that's where God's grace and mercy comes in. 7e helps us to break free from sin and gives us the desire to live 7oly lives.

"The fear of the Lord is the beginning of wisdom."
Proverbs 1:7

Before we can break free from the chains of bondage, we first need to be aware of what can put us in bondage. Fear, doubt, unbelief, guilt, shame, failure or hanging onto hurt are a few examples. Failing in relationships, marriages or jobs can create a chain of failure. It can cause feelings of unworthiness and can block us from stepping out in faith or taking risks for fear of failing again. The chain of failure and the chain of fear of failing needs to be broken to change our mindsets and how we view ourselves. Being under someone else's control and being manipulated by them can put us in bondage. When we're caught in this trap and are being manipulated and controlled by others, we are not allowing ourselves to be led by God's Holy Spirit. In Matt. 6:24 Jesus said, "you cannot serve two masters, you will love the one and hate the other." If we are devoting ourselves to serving another person, we are unable to follow and serve God. We need to be released from obligations that are not of God and the fear or guilt we may feel when we don't do what others think we should be doing.

There's a discontent we feel when we know we aren't in God's will. Something seems to grip us holding us back from being able to move forward and being all God wants us to be or has for us. There can be hindrances and obstacles in our way from seeing God's will and the direction we need to go in to obtain and receive what He has for us. If God is moving in us to go in a different direction that we aren't seeing, we may have to ask Him to breakthrough our old mindsets to open our eyes to see where we are to go. God had to lead the Israelites out of Egypt so He could bring them into the Promised Land (Exodus 14). God may need to take us out of a situation that is not of Him for us to go in a new direction. Taking the step of faith and letting go to believe God for breakthroughs will set us free from the chains of bondage and open our eyes to the truth.

God can take away the doubts and fears and change wrong beliefs that keep us bound and hinder the flow of the Holy Spirit. We can resist change because of fears or unbelief. God wants us to be free and to have healing for our emotional and spiritual scars that can cause us to stay in bondage. When hurts are buried deep, God has to get to the root by unblocking what is buried in our subconscious, bringing past memories to the surface into our awareness. Keeping them buried and hidden can keep us in a state of weakness. Satan will use our weaknesses to cause fear in us when feelings or emotions are triggered through people or circumstances. We can ask God for insights and revelations, to bring memories and past experiences into our awareness, so we can bind them up and be free of them. There can be fears deep within us that can cause us to feel unworthy. We can have a fear of change, of not believing there could be something better for us or we don't feel worthy of it. To get to the root of problems, we need to find out what seeds were planted in our minds and in our hearts that have caused the fear or unworthiness. Once a seed of doubt or fear has been planted in our minds, it can cause us to be drawn into experiences that will cause the fear or doubt to grow, creating a chain of bondage. As God brings things into our awareness, we can bind them up. We will experience freedom in Christ when we are rid of those things that hold us back from truly living and experiencing life the way God intended. God can bring us blessings when we are freed from the chains of bondage that stand in the way of us being able to walk in God's truth and light.

Letting go and giving God control releases His power. It enables us to be led by His Holy Spirit operating under God's strength to have Victory over the enemy. We can never be truly free until we learn to let go and give everything over to God. We have to be open to God, letting Him breakdown walls, barriers or defenses we may have built up so He can deliver us. When the walls come down, God can do the work that needs to be done in our hearts setting us free from the chains that have kept us bound. Every time strongholds are broken, it makes us stronger. When Satan doesn't have a hold on us, his power diminishes. He can only attack us where we are weak. God takes us through experiences to teach us the lessons we need to learn, to make us stronger and to give us more understanding and compassion for others. God doesn't want to see us suffer, but it is so often through suffering we gain insights and understanding and become more aware of the spiritual battles we're in and the strongholds Satan can have over us. There are times our experiences will bring up fears, insecurities and feelings of vulnerability. These things have to be

brought to the surface and acknowledged before God can root them out and bring us the
healing we need. Unless we acknowledge our
weaknesses and submit and release them to
God, we remained unchanged. We won't grow
and get passed those things that hold us back
from being all God designed for us to be. God
strengthens us as we completely let go of the
things we hang onto. The more strongholds we
break free from, the more our eyes of understanding are open. We know Satan is a defeated
foe and we can use the power and authority we
have in Jesus to put him under our feet. We are
less vulnerable to Satan's attacks and it gives
God the freedom to move in our lives and in our
circumstances to bring about what He desires.
We need God's strength and courage to stand
up against the enemy and overcome the battles
to break the chains of bondage.

We can pray on behalf of others to intercede and break the chains of bondage they
maybe under. God will burden our hearts to
pray for someone in bondage. He gives us understanding and the willingness to pray and
fight for them to be set free from the enemy. If
Satan is blinding someone and they are under
deception, we have every right to pray and intercede for them. When we are called to do
spiritual warfare, God may give us a glimpse of
what is in another person's heart to help us to
know how or what to pray to expose the lies of
the enemy or the deception they are under that
can block them from seeing the truth. As we
pray, God breaks down walls and breaks
through obstacles and hindrances standing in

the way and opens the eyes of the person being blinded by the enemy. We will feel a lift in our spirits when God breaks through. Whenever we are obedient to God, praying what 7 e puts on our hearts and intervening on behalf of others, we will see God's glory shown as 7e does a mighty work in other people's hearts and in their lives gaining Victory over the works of the enemy.

The spiritual forces in the heavenly realm are real. We are powerless to fight the spiritual realm without Christ. It is through the power and blood of Jesus that defeats the enemy. We need to exercise our authority in Christ to obtain Victory. Without Christ and God's 7oly Spirit working in us, we fall prey to Satan's lies and deception. It's through Christ and 7is power working in and through us, giving us discernment that we are able to overcome the lies of the devil and break the strongholds he has had over our lives, minds, hearts, spirits, souls, wills and emotions. Our hurts from our past can be overcome, they can be healed and enable us to move forward, but only through the life changing power of God's love. We will experience a peace that goes beyond our understanding (Phil. 4:7) and we'll be content in God when we have been set free. 7e equips us to fight against the spiritual realm through the weapons of warfare and not the weapons of the world. It is through Christ that we are empowered, not in ourselves or through the lies of the enemy.

*For though we live in
the world, we do not wage
war as the world does. The
weapons we fight with are not
the weapons of the world. On the
contrary, they have divine power to
demolish strongholds. We demolish
arguments and every pretension
that sets itself up against the
knowledge of God, and we
take captive every thought
to make it obedient
to Christ.
2 Cor. 10:3-5*

God's plan and purposes will prevail (Proverbs 19:21). He has that awesome power. God spoke and the light overcame the dark (Gen. 1:3). God made the sun and the moon and the stars (Gen. 1:16). Jesus rose from the dead and defeated death (Matt. 2J:6). God has the power to root out the things that are holding us back from receiving His blessings when we allow Him to. Breaking of strongholds exposes the lies of the enemy and reveals the truth. Some lies we have believed can be hidden and buried deep within us that cause us to struggle to move forward, hindering us and stand in the way of our freedom. We need to be free and rid of everything that is not of God. As the Holy Spirit works in us changing us, God can root out everything that is not of Him. God wants what is best for us and wants to change and mold us into the person He has designed for us to be. We limit God when we are hold onto wrong thinking, learned behavior patterns, attitudes and prejudices that keep us blinded to the truth. Breaking down barriers, whether it's been from conditioning, mindsets or attitudes that has kept us in bondage, frees us. When breakthroughs come, we are able to look beyond the natural realm and into the supernatural. We are able to see through God's eyes when we ask Him to show us what we need to see. We will discover who God truly is and be able to live our lives free in Him. We will have revelation, knowledge, power and authority to walk free in Christ when we know our God, His character and who He is and take hold of that truth to see how awesome His power truly is. We can live free in Christ when we have broken free from the chains of bondage and the strongholds that have kept us bound.

Chapter 17

Be Healed, Transformed & Stronger in the Lord

We become stronger in the Lord when we've been set free. Learning to walk with the Lord and not compromising our values or faith gives us strength, freedom and Victory. When we've broken free and are healed, our faith increases giving us more awareness and understanding of how powerful God really is. As the truth of how powerful our God is (7eb. 11:3,7, 29,30) sinks into our hearts and spirits, we can know and truly believe that nothing is impossible for God (Luke 1:37) and that we can do all things through Christ that strengthens us (Phil. 4:13). God wants to raise us up to be true warriors and to be mighty vessels for 7im to work through. Emotional healing gives us confidence and courage to move forward in God, standing firm in our faith to win the Victory. We become more effective Christians, bringing others into the Kingdom to see them saved and set free. When we live in God's truth, we learn to discern and can see through the lies and deception the enemy tries to blind us with.

There are many examples in the Bible of how God demonstrates 7is power. In the book of Joshua, God dried up the Jordan River so all the peoples of the earth might know that the hand of the Lord is powerful and that they might always fear the Lord their God (Joshua 4:23,24). The fear of the Lord is the beginning of knowledge (Proverbs. 1:7). It is acknowledging and recognizing the awesomeness of God and grasping hold of what a Mighty God 7e is and what 7e can do. When we don't have the fear of the Lord in us, we lack the understanding and we struggle to trust and believe. When the fear of the Lord is in us, we no longer have a fear of man. We know the awesomeness of God and that 7e has the power and authority over all things. In Joshua 6:16-20, the walls of Jericho fell and God gave the city to the Israelites and told them that all that was in it was to be devoted to the Lord. God gave the Israelites a warning to keep away from the devoted things, so that they will not bring on their own destruction by taking any of the silver, gold, bronze and iron that were sacred to the Lord. God speaks to Joshua saying,

"Israel has sinned; they
have violated my covenant,
which I commanded them to
keep. They have taken some
of the devoted things; they have
stolen, they have lied, they have
put them with their own possessions.
That is why the Israelites cannot
stand against their enemies; they
turn their backs and run because
they have been made liable to
destruction. I will not be with
you anymore unless you

> *destroy whatever among*
> *you is devoted to*
> *destruction."*
> Joshua 7:11,12

In other words, God is explaining to them that they've opened themselves up to the enemy by turning from God and disobeying 7im. We need to destroy the idols in our lives that stand in the way between God and us that keeps us from being completely devoted to the Lord. God warns us in Joshua:

> *"But be very careful to*
> *keep the commandment*
> *and the law that Moses the*
> *servant of the Lord gave you:*
> *to love the Lord your God, to*
> *walk in all his ways, to obey his*
> *commands, to hold fast to him*
> *and to serve him with all*
> *your heart and all*
> *your soul."*
> Joshua 22:5

Being truly devoted to the Lord and submitting ourselves completely to 7im allows God to set us apart for 7im to do the mighty work 7e has for us to do, to defeat the works of the enemy and to bring others into the Kingdom. Being in a right relationship with Christ makes us stronger in the Lord and cleanses us from all unrighteousness, giving us the power and authority over the enemy to free us and others from bondage. We can have Victory in Jesus wh;n w; ar; d;vot;d to God, d;stroyi ng th; works of th; ; n; my, so Satan can no long;r hold anything against us. In Joshua 14:9, God gav; Joshua th; land as his inh; ritanc; and for his childr;n b;caus; h; follow;d th; Lord whol;h;art;dly. Joshua claims in 14:11, "I am still as strong today as th; day Mos;s s;nt m; out; I'm just as vigorous to go out to battl; now as I was th; n." Joshua 21:44,45 stat; s, Not on; of th;ir ;n;mi;s withstood th;m; th; Lord hand;d all th;ir ;n;mi;s ov;r to th;m. Not on; of all th; Lord's good promis; s to th; hous; of Isra;l fail; d; ; v; ry on; was fulfill; d. It ; ncour-ag;s us to know God k; ; ps His Word and what H; has spok;n will com; to pass.

My word that goes out
from my mouth: It will not
return to me empty, but will
accomplish what I desire and
achieve the purpose for
which I sent it.
Isaiah 55:11

Wh;n w; truly b;li; v; God and tak; Him at His Word, it incr; as; s our trust and faith, making us strong;r in Him. God giv;s us th; str;ngth to do th; work H; calls us to do as long as w; trust, b; li; v; and follow Him with all our h;arts. Without b;li;f in th; Lord, th;r; is no Victory b;caus; our sinful, unb;li;vin g h;arts turn us away from th; living God (H; b. 3:12). W; can allow f; ar and unb; li; f to d; stroy and d;f;at us or w; can ask God to chang; our h;arts of unb;li;f to on; that b;li;v; s completely in Him.

When we love the Lord with all our hearts and souls, we are more willing to give our wills over to Him. Letting go of our wills allows God to move freely through us breaking through the lies of the enemy and the strongholds he has had over us. Breaking bondages over our lives frees us, builds our faith and brings us into more knowledge and a greater understanding of God. The more of ourselves we give to God, the deeper our walk becomes and the more we mature in the Lord. As we grow and change through experiences and circumstances, even through hurt and pain, we can gain understanding of how God can use what we've gone through to prepare us for what's ahead. God takes us through trials and a training period making us stronger to equip us to do the work He has for us to do. He gives us the power and authority over the enemy to win the battles. Whenever we do anything for God, it's wise to pray a blood covering over our loved ones and ourselves to keep us safe and protected against the enemy. Moses felt doubt and was humbled before God. He wondered how could a man like him be used of God (Exodus 3:11). We can all be used by God to bring glory to His Name if we believe it and step out in faith. It may mean giving up what we want or think we want to be led by God's Holy Spirit, but in doing so we will see God's glory and be blessed beyond what we could even imagine (1 Cor. 2:9).

"I have given you
authority to trample on

160

*snakes and scorpions and
to over-come all the power
of the enemy; nothing
will harm you."
Luke: 10: 19*

As we grow in the Lord so do our gifts. God may give us the gift of being a prayer warrior to pray for others so their hearts can be opened and softened to receive Jesus as their Lord and Savior. We can share the Word of God, but if hearts aren't open to receive, it can fall on deaf ears. Prayer lays the foundation so God can work and seeds can be planted when we are called to share the Word. As we mature, we gain a deeper understanding and are better prepared to use God's gifts properly, giving glory to 7is Name. As we gain more wisdom and understanding of the Lord, it increases our knowledge of 7im and as we go deeper in God, we are able to receive and gain insights to prophecy and dreams and revelations. We are better able to discern and not fall under deception or distort God's truth. As we grow stronger in the Lord we are also able to recognize the subtle snares of the devil and not fall into the trap of pride or believing lies of the enemy that it's our power and not the Lords. We will have the assurance that the peace of God, which transcends all understanding, will guard our hearts and minds in Christ Jesus (Phil. 4:7). God's perfect love casts out all fear (1 John 4:1J), but it also breaks down barriers, shatters defenses and walls we can put up and hide behind. God's love will never cease or fail or stop

161

loving (1 Cor. 13:8). God's perfect love will never reject, cause fear or turn away anyone that willingly comes to Christ. His perfect love will always accept and forgive and show compassion, mercy and understanding. God wants to put the perfect love He has for mankind in all of us, so we can show His love to others, leading them to salvation.

As Christians we will not be able to escape the trials and spiritual battles in this life. God may call us to do battle against the enemy to fulfill a certain purpose He wants to accomplish. Going through a spiritual battle can be difficult at times as we struggle against doubts and fears and are plagued by feelings of unworthiness. There will be times we feel we've gained ground and have won the battle only to find there are more things we need to go through or to break free from before we see an end to the spiritual battle we are in. We can grow weary when the time drags on and we face more challenges to overcome. We can go through times of suffering as we fight a spiritual battle to have what God desires for us. When we are faced with adversity and trials, we can discover more of who we are and what we're truly made of. Going through trials helps us become stronger as we are drawn into a closer walk with God. There is an inner strength we draw from when we're going through trials and tribulations that we may never knew existed. We draw closer to God as we learn to lean on Him for strength and guidance. We gain Victory as we learn to fight against the enemy through our prayers and spiritual warfare. God will give us insights and understanding as we persevere and keep praying. There is a sense of relief when the battle is over and we are changed. Even though it can be difficult going through the battles, we come out stronger and more resilient at the end of it. We can gain more understanding of why we had to go through what we did to see God's plan come to pass. It gives us a greater appreciation when we receive God's blessings and have what we've been waiting and fighting for. God will often put two people together, each with their own unique gifts and strengths to work together to make a powerful difference in other people's lives. When God joins two people together, united under the blood of Jesus and they are following and being obedient to God and submitting to His will, they can accomplish much for His Kingdom. God didn't send Moses out alone to free the Israelites. God sent his brother, Aaron (Exodus 4:15) to be with Moses to help him to speak to the Israelites. God encouraged Moses letting him know He would help them to know what to say and teach them what they needed to do. Ecclesiastes 4:12, "Though one may be overpowered, two can defend themselves. A cord of three strands is not quickly broken." The third strand is God at the center. When we're doing what God calls us to do, we are going to come up against spiritual opposition and Satan's attacks. When two are working together, they can be an emotional and spiritual support and strength for each other and have more power to stand against the enemy to defeat him. We can do mighty works through Christ and His power and strength breaking through strongholds and bondages, setting the captives free.

God has so much 7e wants to give us. Living in a fallen world, there are times our flesh will fight against our spirits (Gal. 5:17). We need to be emptied of self, to be filled with more of Jesus to win the battle. It means dieing to self so we can become a mighty force in Christ to come against and defeat the enemy of our souls. Dieing to self is doing what God wants and letting 7im have 7is way, letting go of all our perceived notions and wrong beliefs. It's being willing to sacrifice whatever God asks of us, laying our own agendas aside and what we think we want, to do what God knows is best for us and to see 7is plan and purpose fulfilled. God's ways are always better. All we need is a willing heart to become vessels for God to use us for 7is divine purposes to accomplish what 7e desires. When we die to self, we will no longer believe the lies of the enemy that we aren't good enough or worthy enough to be used by God. Our thinking changes and we become more spiritually aware and have a greater understanding of God. God will work in us to help us to believe the truth and to be all 7e has created and designed for us to be. As we learn to lean on God and not on ourselves, God gives us the strength and courage and the ability to accomplish what 7e calls us to do. It's God working through us that changes our hearts, giving us what we need to help others to be free from the enemy's grip. God wants us to be healed and made whole in 7im and to be set free and in doing so we can help others, showing them the way to freedom, healing and wholeness. Lives change through receiving salvation through Christ and experiencing God's love. The more we give ourselves over to God, the more we will see changes in our lives and in the lives of people He puts on our hearts to pray for. As our lives are transformed through the power and love of Jesus, we can have inner healing from past hurts, be freed from bondage, know God's will for our lives and be stronger in the Lord. What better way to show God's glory as we allow Him to transform us into the people He has created us to be and to follow His will and calling. As long as we are willing vessels, being obedient to God, we will fulfill His plan and purpose and see others set free, helping them to discover the powerful love God has for each and every one of us. Knowing God and His character helps build our trust and faith in Him as strongholds break and distorted thinking and wrong beliefs are changed. As God's truth seeps deep down into our innermost being and our minds are renewed with the mind of Christ, we can learn to live in Victory as we are transformed into the people of God He has destined for us to be.

Printed in the United States
by Baker & Taylor Publisher Services